Technological Competency as Caring in Nursing: A Model for Practice

By Rozzano C. Locsin, RN, PhD

Books Published by the Honor Society of Nursing, Sigma Theta Tau International

Making a Difference: Stories from the Point of Care, Volume I, Hudacek, 2005.

Making a Difference: Stories from the Point of Care, Volume II, Hudacek, 2004.

A Daybook for Nurses: Making a Difference Each Day, Hudacek, 2004.

Pivotal Moments in Nursing: Leaders Who Changed the Path of a Profession, Houser and Player, 2004.

Building and Managing a Career in Nursing: Strategies for Advancing Your Career, Miller, 2003.

Collaboration for the Promotion of Nursing, Briggs, Merk, and Mitchell, 2003.

Ordinary People, Extraordinary Lives: The Stories of Nurses, Smeltzer and Vlasses, 2003.

The HeART of Nursing: Expressions of Creative Art in Nursing, Wendler, 2002.

Stories of Family Caregiving: Reconsideration of Theory, Literature, and Life, Poirier and Ayres, 2002.

As We See Ourselves: Jewish Women in Nursing, Benson, 2001.

Cadet Nurse Stories: The Call for and Response of Women During World War II, Perry and Robinson, 2001.

Creating Responsive Solutions to Healthcare Change, McCullough, 2001.

Nurses' Moral Practice: Investing and Discounting Self, Kelly, 2000.

Nursing and Philanthropy: An Energizing Metaphor for the 21st Century, McBride, 2000.

Gerontological Nursing Issues for the 21st Century, Gueldner and Poon, 1999.

The Roy Adaptation Model-Based Research: 25 Years of Contributions to Nursing Science, Boston Based Adaptation Research in Nursing Society, 1999.

The Adventurous Years: Leaders in Action 1973-1999, Henderson, 1998.

Immigrant Women and Their Health: An Olive Paper, Ibrahim, Meleis, Lipson, Muecke, and Smith, 1998.

The Neuman Systems Model and Nursing Education: Teaching Strategies and Outcomes, Lowry, 1998.

The Image Editors: Mind, Spirit, and Voice, Hamilton, 1997.

The Language of Nursing Theory and Metatheory, King and Fawcett, 1997.

Virginia Avenel Henderson: Signature for Nursing, Hermann, 1997.

For more information and to order these books from the Honor Society of Nursing, Sigma Theta Tau International, visit the society's Web site at **www.nursingsociety.org/publications**, or go to **www.nursingknowledge.org/stti/books**, the Web site of Nursing Knowledge International, the honor society's sales and distribution division, or call 1.888.NKI.4.YOU (U.S. and Canada) or +1.317.634.8171 (Outside U.S. and Canada).

Technological Competency as Caring in Nursing: A Model for Practice

By Rozzano C. Locsin, RN, PhD
and contributors

 Sigma Theta Tau International
Honor Society of Nursing
Indianapolis, Indiana, USA

RT
42
L63
2005

Sigma Theta Tau International

Editor-in-Chief: Jeff Burnham
Acquisitions Editor: Fay L. Bower, RN, DNSc, FAAN
Editor: Carla Hall
Indexter: Angela Bess, RN

Interior Design and Composition: Rebecca Harmon

Printed in the United States of America
Printing and Binding by V.G. Reed & Sons

Sigma Theta Tau International
550 West North Street
Indianapolis, IN 46202

Visit our Web site at **www.nursingknowledge.org/stti/books** for more information on our books.

ISBN: 1-930538-12-X

Library of Congress Cataloging-in-Publication Data

Locsin, Rozzano C., 1954-
  Technological competency as caring in nursing : a model for practice / Rozzano Locsin and contributors.
     p. ; cm.
  Includes bibliographical references and index.
  ISBN 1-930538-12-X
  1. Nursing. 2. Caring. 3. Medical technology. 4. Nursing—Technological innovations. 5. Nurse and patient.
  [DNLM: 1. Nursing Care—methods. 2. Biomedical Technology. 3. Clinical Competence. 4. Models, Nursing. 5. Nurse-Patient Relations. 6. Nursing Theory. WY 100 L818t 2005] I. Sigma Theta Tau International. II. Title.

RT42.L63 2005
610.73—dc22

                                                                    2005003749

ACKNOWLEDGMENTS

The publication of this book highlights my struggle to understand nursing as a discipline of knowledge and as a practice profession. It has been a long and extensive wait ... and it continues.

Essential to this understanding are outstanding theoreticians and scholars of nursing: Savina Schoenhofer and Anne Boykin continue to challenge my knowledge of nursing and of the uniqueness of Nursing as Caring as a model for practice; Marguerite Purnell shares her passion for nursing and continues to inspire; Marilyn Parker's scholarship of practice immensely influences my commitment to theory-based practice; Alan Barnard and Ruth McCaffrey who are exceptional colleagues and sustained knowers; Marilyn Suasin-Juergens who continues to practice nursing and is a treasured friend; and to Marion Goddard and Loren Nedelman whose experiences with technological competency as caring make knowing persons live meaningfully in nursing.

I remain grateful to Fay Bower, acquisitions editor, Carla Hall, development editor, and Jeff Burnham, publisher, of The Honor Society of Nursing, Sigma Theta Tau International. The journey makes the product most meaningful.

Rozzano C. Locsin

COPYRIGHT ACKNOWLEDGMENTS

The author and publisher gratefully acknowledge permission to reprint material used within the text of chapters within this book:

Locsin, R. (1995). Machine technologies and caring in nursing. *Image: Journal of Nursing Scholarship, 26*(2), 201-203.

Locsin, R. (1998). Technological competency as expression of caring in critical care nursing. *Holistic Nursing Practice, 12*(4), 51-56.

Locsin, R. (2001). Practicing nursing: Technological competency as an expression of caring in nursing. In Locsin, R., (2001) (ed). *Advancing technology, caring, and nursing.* Westport, CT: Auburn House.

Locsin, R. (2005). Technological competency as caring in nursing: Knowing persons as process of nursing. In Parker, M. (2005). *Nursing Theories for Nursing Practice.* Phila: F.A. Davis, Co. (in press).

Table of Contents

Foreword

From early nursing history—in biblical references, military references, references to Nightingale, and modern nursing—two ideas coexist and extend into the present. One is the idea of nursing as a human expression of loving kindness, or caring; the second is the idea of loving kindness or the caring that is nursing being mediated through instrumental technology. Competently offering a wounded soldier a sip of nourishing and warming broth from a clean utensil—this is a simple example of technological competency as caring in nursing that reaches from the dim past right into the present, and no doubt into the foreseeable future. Another example, more modern but no more immediate, is being with, comforting, and safeguarding the person through vigilant monitoring and proper adjustment of the renal dialysis machine used by the patient with kidney failure. How is it that both are examples of the caring that is nursing?

In this book, Dr. Locsin has brought together these two ideas that are central to our understanding of nursing as a practical human service of caring. His early work to integrate the ideas of technological competence and caring, ideas that had somehow come to be addressed as oppositional values in nursing, was initially published under the title "Machine Technologies and Caring in Nursing" (Locsin, 1995). Locsin's early scholarship in this arena was grounded in Boykin and Schoenhofer's (1993) theory of Nursing as Caring, Sandelowski's (1993) theoretical formulation of technological dependency in nursing, and Ray's (1987) technological caring in critical care nursing. This book builds on Locsin's (2001) earlier edited volume that brought international scholars together around key concepts of caring, technology, and nursing in an effort to stimulate thinking toward reintegration of those concepts.

A segment of the nursing literature on caring makes it clear that knowledgeable and competent "doing for" remains—for nurses and patients—an essential characteristic of nursing. See, for example, the reports of studies using Larson's (1984; 1986; 1987) Care-Q instruments, Wolf's Caring Behaviors Inventory (Green, 2004; Wolf et al., 1994), Cronin and Harrison's (1988) Caring Behaviors Assessment (Dorsey,

Phillips & Williams, 2001) and others. What some call instrumental caring is always ranked at or near the top when patients are asked to rate their preferences for the way nurses express caring. Nurses expect to express their nursing in action, much of that action involving the use of biomedical and other technology on behalf of their patients. Patients and their families continue to rank knowledgeable, skillful "doing for" as a high expectation from nurses. For a time in nursing, we seemed to have placed ourselves in a position of advocating "either/or"—either high tech or high touch—even though thoughtful nurses knew in their hearts that this was a false dichotomy. Locsin's model of technological competency as caring in nursing opens the door for a practical and supportable understanding of how the either/or dilemma might be not only resolved but transcended as well. The Locsin model demonstrates the "right relationship" between technology and caring in nursing by making clear that the competent use of technology in nursing is in service to caring. No longer is it a matter of either caring or technology. No longer is it fully supportable to claim "no time to care."

The idea of intentionality is the explicit link between technology and caring in nursing. When technology is employed competently in nursing situations as an intentional expression of caring in nursing, the troublesome dichotomies disappear. I was recently in conversation with a person who is the administrator of nursing services in a hospice. He was in the process of exploring the theory of Nursing as Caring as a potential framework for a practice model that would keep "being with" at the center of nursing in his setting. When I recommended that he include the Locsin model of technological competency as caring in nursing in his exploration of nursing as caring, and offered a brief description of the model, he immediately responded with an "aha." The artificial dichotomy with which the hospice nursing administrator and staff were struggling—either caring or technology—gave way to a powerful conceptual integration that made practical sense and offered immediate direction for the improvement of care.

Any general theory of nursing relies on the development of compatible, systematically-developed, middle-range theories for its practical implementation. The Locsin model makes a significant contribution to the feasibility of the theory of Nursing as Caring as a transformative vehicle for nursing. Locsin's work is obviously guided by the question asked by thoughtful nurses everywhere: How can I satisfactorily reconcile the idea of competent use of technology with the idea of caring in nursing? The chapters in this book significantly embellish a practical understanding of the solution offered by the Locsin model, and indeed, enrich the practical value of all of the general theories of nursing that are grounded in caring.

Savina O. Schoenhofer, Ph.D., RN
Professor, Department of Graduate Nursing
Alcorn State University, Natchez, Mississippi

REFERENCES

Boykin, A., & Schoenhofer, S. (1993). *Nursing as caring: A model for transforming practice.* New York: National League for Nursing

Dorsey, C., Phillips, K. D., & Williams, C. (2004). Adult sickle cell patients' perceptions of nurses' caring behaviors. *ABNF Journal,* Sep-Oct;12(5), 95-100

Green, A. (2004). Caring behaviors as perceived by nurse practitioners. *J Am Acad Nurse Pract.* Jul, 16(7), 283-90.

Larson P. (1984). Important nurse caring behaviours perceived by patients with cancer. *Oncology Nursing Forum,* 11(6), 40-46.

Larson P. (1986). Cancer nurses' perceptions of caring. *Cancer Nursing,* 9(2), 86-91.

Larson P. (1987). Comparison of cancer patients' and professional nurses' perceptions of important nurse caring behaviors. *Heart and Lung,* 16(2), 187-193.

Locsin, R. C. (2001). Advancing technology, caring, and nursing. Westport, CT: Auburn House.

Locsin, R. C. (1995). Machine technologies and caring in nursing. *Image: J Nurs Scholarship,* 27(3), 201-3.

Ray, M.A. (1987). Technological caring: A new model in critical care. *Dimensions in Critical Care Nursing,* 6(3), 166-73.

Sandelowski, M. (1993). Toward a theory of technology dependency. Nursing Outlook, 41(1), 36-42

Wolf, Z. R., Giardino, E. R., Osborne, P. A., & Ambrose, M. S. (1994). Dimensions of nurse caring. *Image J Nurs Scholarship,* 26(2), 107-11.

PROLOGUE

Philosophical movements introduce new perspectives that promote changes in nursing processes and practices. While caring is not unique to nursing, it is a major part of nursing and demonstrates the ability of philosophy to ground a practice. Given this, it is of great importance that from a caring perspective this philosophical perspective is developed into a theoretical perspective. This book attempts to expand the practicality of the caring perspective as foundational to the critical and legitimate practice of professional nursing.

The study of nursing evolved from a traditional apprenticeship to a generalized practice using the knowledge of biomedicine and the idea that patients need fixing and need to be made whole again. Today, the evolving knowledge from this perspective, in consonance with dominant philosophical movements, has fostered a knowledge-based practice that is derived from theoretical perspectives. One such theory is described in the book *Nursing as Caring: A Model for Transforming Practice* by Boykin and Schoenhofer (2001). Driving this theory as the basis of practice is the idea that to be human is to be caring, that persons are caring by virtue of their humanness, and that nursing is nurturing persons living caring and growing in caring (Boykin and Schoenhofer, 2001).

Boykin and Schoenhofer (2001) link nursing and technology. They believe there are many ways this linkage is evident. One is the appreciation of *technological competency as caring*. Although nursing technologies are understood in many ways, the idea of technological competency as caring in nursing is fairly new. It proposes a model of practice whereby a nurse, one who is technologically competent, is understood and appreciated as a caring nurse. The nurse's technological competency is thus an actual expression of caring in nursing.

PREFACE

A quintessential question often asked of nurse scholars, theoreticians, academicians, and practitioners of nursing is: What is the pertinence of theories of nursing? Critical to this question is the concern for the value of nursing theories as a guide for practice. The English word "theory" is derived from the Greek word, "theoria" which means "to see," a way of revealing phenomena that is previously hidden from one's awareness (Watson, 1999). The pertinence of theories of nursing becomes an issue when the profession of nursing is viewed simply as a practice using technologies in various healthcare settings. It is not unusual for healthcare practice professions to emphasize the understanding of patients as predictable, fixable, and curable through available technologies. Nursing as a discipline and professional practice builds its worth primarily from aspects of caring that are shaped from knowing persons who are whole and complete in the moment. Such nursing encourages creativity, innovation, and imagination as an informed and knowledgeable practice.

Should There be More Practice Theories to Guide Nursing?

I believe that theories of nursing are derived from varying worldviews that can easily provide practice theories to guide professional nursing. However, is there a need for another middle-range theoretical or practice model for nursing?

Personal Thoughts

I used to think that the practice of nursing was simply nurses conforming to the ways of traditional, vocational, and regimented procedures, such as following patient-care orders. Then I began to question the disciplinary and professional bases for nursing practice, realizing that there must be a more educated reason for the practice of professional nursing, and with it a practice framework derived from a body of knowledge that is of nursing.

Eventually, these questioning thoughts were replaced by the appreciation of the existence of extant theories of nursing. What I soon realized was that, indeed, nursing is a distinct discipline of knowledge and is a professional practice. Guiding the practice of nursing are extant theories of nursing requiring calculated thinking reflecting the critical appreciation of people as whole or complete in the moment.

Nursing is a knowledgeable practice. The ontology of nursing underscores its nature, value, and consequent practice. A bona fide description of nursing and the ensuing process or knowledge sustains the appreciation of theoretical bases of nursing practices. One of these descriptions of nursing is the recognition of technological competency as caring in nursing. It is a practice model that advances the consideration of proficiency with technologies for knowing individuals, a practice of nursing guided by the general theory of nursing as caring (Boykin & Schoenhofer, 2001).

Armed with these thoughts, I found that what was critical to nursing knowledge were answers to questions, such as "what makes nursing knowledge uniquely nursing knowledge?" Earlier in my practice, I was convinced that there was really nothing in nursing that was exclusive to nursing. What I used in my nursing practice was biomedical information—knowledge gained from other healthcare disciplines such as anatomy, physiology, pathologic physiology, biochemistry, and so on. Interestingly, this was intriguing and informing to me to know that as a nurse I can practice nursing using knowledge from various disciplines and that I can predict and prescribe the best nursing care possible based upon this body of knowledge. Nevertheless, the question remained, "Was I nursing?"

This book is in three parts. Part I, chapters 1-5, describes the conceptualizations of technological competency, caring, and nursing. Part II, chapters 6-8, illustrates practice issues inherent in the model and encourages further dialogue about the conceptualizations of technological competency as caring in nursing. Part III, chapters 9-11, contains practice descriptions of care situations in which the distinctive process of nursing guided by technological competency as caring is used. Although the intention is for a sectional format, this book certainly unfolds as one, true to the mind-set of continuity of understanding people as whole in the moment.

The following are ontological and epistemological questions of nursing that are designed to enhance the appreciation of the tension between practicing nursing and the practice of nursing as viewed from another disciplinary perspective:

- Should nursing knowledge be grounded in empirical data?
- Should nursing be like medicine? If so, why?
- Should nursing *not* be like medicine? If so, why?
- Is the focus of nursing the health or wellness of the patient?
- In attempting to attain, maintain, and sustain the health and wellness of patients, do nurses need to understand what it is like to be a person?
- Are nurses meeting the desired outcomes of attaining, maintaining, and sustaining the health and wellness of patients when they practice like physicians?
- From an advanced perspective of nursing as medicine, can the nurse provide healthcare from a more affordable position?
- If nursing is like medicine; if nursing practice is like medical practice; if by this practice the nurse focuses on the person as whole and complete in the moment and is able to attain, maintain, and sustain the health and well-being of the person, is the nurse nursing?
- If the nurse is nursing, the patient is being nursed, and the health and wellness of the patient and the nurse is attained, maintained, and sustained, then is nursing meeting the societal need of a profession? Of a service profession?

This book is an affirmation of nursing, a discipline and a profession with a substantive body of knowledge supporting its practice. Caring is the essence of nursing, the underlying appreciation of experience within human health. In recognizing the value of nursing as a professional practice with a substantive body of knowledge grounding its practice, its focus is the person who is whole, complete, dynamic, unpredictable, and complete in the moment.

Nursing practice involves continuous knowing of human beings as whole and complete in the moment. The concept of wholeness is not limited to the comprehension of human beings as a composite of organ systems. It is the appreciation of human beings as always whole who are hoping, dreaming, and aspiring uniquely moment to moment. Persons appreciate life fully and exclusively in the moment. Understanding nursing and appreciating the person requires that the nurse affirms and celebrates persons as whole. Technologies in nursing as mechanisms of knowing enhance the efficacy of understanding persons as whole and complete in the moment. Technologies in nursing include means through which the nurse can respond to patients' calls for affirmation and celebration of the fullness of their lives.

Technological competency—the competent use of technologies in nursing—is the proficient expression of nursing by nurses who know persons as whole and complete in the moment. The process of knowing persons is the continuous appreciation of people as whole human beings. Continuous knowing entails calling forth available processes and other innovative, creative, and imaginative efforts. One of these available processes is the popular and traditional nursing process of assessment, intervention, and evaluation. In general, processes of nursing allow the continuous, circular appreciation of conditions and situations that affirm people as whole and complete in the moment. True to technological competency as caring in nursing is the appreciation of knowing persons as whole in the moment. Critical to the use of the traditional nursing process is the understanding that its use does not constitute the all-encompassing process. Its use allows the nurse to know "what is" the person, a limited view of the person as a composite. A critical situation that calls forth this opportunity is when a person is unconscious or in a life-threatening situation.

Knowing persons as a practice of nursing requires knowing "what" and "who" the person is. Of greater importance to knowing persons is the condition that it is the person's wish to be known that is critical to the practice of nursing. This wish is communicated to the nurse. Doing so, the person allows the nurse to enter the other's world (Boykin & Schoenhofer, 2001). Nursing requires knowledge about the "what" and "who" of the person. Perpetuating the use of the traditional nursing process of assessment and intervention does not serve well the practice of nursing.

The Practice Model

The recognition of theories of nursing as guides to practice, and the desire to ground practice from a view that is of nursing, are clearly delineated and supported by nursing scholars, theoreticians, and intellectuals. Theories of nursing are intended to explain, predict, describe, and prescribe. Found in these theories are ways to maintain a singularity in which the person as whole remains the focus of the theories rather than aspects of the composite human—the one prescribed by biological, behavioral, and medical theories. From the early theories and concepts of nursing, including nursing as a helping art by Wiedenbach (1964), the appreciation of a practice discipline began with a framework guiding the outcomes of care.

Therefore, I'll ask again: Is there a need for yet another middle-range theoretical model or practice model for nursing? For many practical reasons, a practice model that is designed to describe, predict, explain, and prescribe its practice is necessary to account for a professional practice with a knowledge base that is uniquely established on abstract knowledge. Likewise, the continuing advancement of technology in healthcare and the consequent demands for nurses to be technologically adept at manipulating technologies—and in designing techniques and efficient ways of practicing nursing—underscores the need for practice models of nursing. As a model of practice, technological competency as caring in nursing is timely. Notably, such a model legitimizes and honors nursing practice as critical to human health.

Important to the appreciation of this model of practice is the awareness of the concepts within which it is fashioned. The concept of persons as whole is derived from views of persons as ever changing, dynamic, growing, living, and unpredictable regardless of composition. In this conception, the comprehension of person or persons includes the concept of "patient" from a biomedical view—or, the nurse and the one nursed. Critical to this conception is the understanding that persons are appreciated as whole and complete in the moment and that they do not need fixing or to be made "whole" again.

References

Boykin, A., & Schoenhofer, S. (2001). *Nursing as caring: A model for transforming practice*. New York: Jones & Bartlett, National League for Nursing.

Wiedenbach, E. (1964). *Clinical nursing: A helping art*. New York: Springer.

A WORD PICTURE OF LIFE'S MEANINGS

Archetypal memory of being broken
Like a shattered mirror.
However we tend to focus on our broken edges
Rather than the perfect light we reflect.
We also tend to focus on the shape and size
Of the various pieces,
Not realizing that it is our brokenness that makes us whole.
We are made whole in relationship to one another,
As one broken edge fits seamlessly with other edges.
Those who cannot tolerate their sense of brokenness
Hide in darkness where they reflect darkness
And can no longer see how they fit into the scheme of it.
Or we laboriously file away at our broken edges.
However, just as we imagine
We find perfection in community,
We fear loss of identity in sameness.
It is then we discover multidimensionality
Realizing that our individual light-reflecting surfaces
Are facets of a diamond.
We discover the approximation of facet edges
Is as important as the facets themselves.
In the brilliance of a diamond where every edge
Is entirely unique in relation to all the other edges.

—Patrick Dean

PART

1

Conceptualizations of Technological Competency, Caring, and Nursing

"Technological competency as caring in nursing as a conceptual model occurs when caring and technologies in nursing coexist. The harmonization of these concepts places the practice of nursing within the context of modern healthcare and acknowledges that both concepts can co-exist."

1

CHAPTER

An Introduction to the Theory of Technological Competency of Caring

By Rozzano C. Locsin

For some nurses, the care of patients has become dependent on expert usage of machine technology. These nurses often claim nursing routines in intensive care units have become so overwhelmingly machine-oriented the nurses can no longer care for patients. Many of the activities focus on ventilators, cardiac monitors, or documentation requirements that keep the nurse from the practice of nursing. In the views of these nurses, talking to patients and families is seen as superfluous and seldom is viewed as a nursing priority. Caring activities such as "being with" a patient are viewed as time spent in unnecessary activities because these activities do not influence the patient's health and are therefore expendable. They require nursing time but have no immediate, identifiable outcome.

The following story described by one nurse recalls her experience practicing nursing in an intensive care unit and supports the belief that nursing care is becoming more about technology management than about caring for the person.

A major turning point in my career came when I took care of a patient who had cardiomyopathy. He was in his early fifties, needed a heart transplant, was critically ill, and was very unstable. He was on a respirator, along with all kinds of devices and catheters attached to his body. In addition, he had a device called LVAD (Left Ventricular Assistive Device). All critical care nurses are given a course on taking care of patients with an LVAD. Attached to his chest were large tubes. He received more than one hundred units of blood products, and multiple emergency medications and liters of fluid were administered to him. He was rushed to the operating room each day of his confinement. His body systems failed one by one. There was no sign that his body responded positively to anything done to him. We lost him, although from the beginning he was not expected to live long. I cannot imagine how the patient and his family perceived the whole situation. The patient no longer looked like he did when he arrived. When I looked at him I thought "what have we done to this man?" From that moment on, my perspective changed. I felt that working around so many machines was pulling me away from nursing. The focus in patient care was shifting. I was afraid of becoming procedure-centered—afraid of becoming a machine myself. The force behind advancing technology was so strong; I was being engulfed by it. This was unfortunate, but true. I wanted out.

Leaving the critical care unit was my declaration that I did not want to deal with another device, button, switch, or parts of machines that patients come into contact with so that I could provide "quality" patient care. And, please forgive my analogy, but when all kinds of tubes and hoses are hooked up to my patients, the vision of an octopus comes to my mind. Its tentacles are obstructing my way. I used to ask myself "where is the patient I am entrusted to care for?" (Juergens, 2001, personal communication).

This vignette shows the importance of technologies in nursing practice settings and the increasing demands that these technologies place on nurses. Demands such as these create nursing experiences that cause the nurse to question the value of a practice that was intended to provide human care but that has become more about the administration of technology.

From a practice perspective, all nursing models, theories, and conceptual frameworks are considered bases for practice. However, caring in nursing practice is the essence of the human health experience (Newman, Sime, & Corcoran-Perry, 1991) and an important element of a patient's well being. Likewise, nursing knowledge development and practice are based on varying perspectives. There is a continued effort to encourage the proliferation of various nursing models in forming a nursing practice rather than building that practice from a singular perspective such as a mechanistic or humanistic view.

Traditional Models of Nursing: The Nursing Process

Derived from theoretical frameworks that have evolved from philosophical perspectives popular long ago, nursing practitioners today subscribe to the traditional nursing process as the best practical guide for the delivery of nursing care. Contemporary application of this process by nurse practitioners, who have deliberately increased its use by prescribing functions involving diagnosis and treatments from a clinical health model, has expanded the prescriptive and predictive process of nursing. Unfortunately, the traditional nursing process, which includes assessment, planning, intervention, and evaluation, limits the appreciation of human beings as persons. It provides care for human beings based upon the evidence-and-cure process in which nursing functions are narrowly described as the diagnosis and treatment of disease and the administration of medication.

> Competency with technology is the skilled demonstration of intentional, deliberate, and authentic activities by experienced nurses who practice in environments requiring technological expertise.

Technological Competency as Caring: A New Model

Technological competency as caring in nursing is a conceptual model that presents the link between technology and caring in nursing as coexisting harmoniously. According to Locsin (1995), the concepts of technology and caring within the context of competency illustrate the realities of advancing technologies in healthcare. From this perspective, this conceptual model is a situation-specific model that delineates the practice of nursing and the relatedness between technology, caring, and nursing.

The practice model that is crucial to contemporary nursing is one where the practice of caring in nursing can be expressed through technological competency. This practice model proposes that both high-technology and competency with technology are vital to the practice of contemporary nursing. Competency with technology is the skilled demonstration of intentional and authentic activities by experienced nurses who practice in environments requiring technological expertise. Fundamental to technological competency in contemporary nursing practice is the deliberate and continuous use of technologies in nursing for the purpose of knowing persons.

Often, technological competency is viewed as the opposite of caring. However, these two concepts—traditional caring and technological competency as caring—have a relationship that is critical to nursing practice. Harmonizing these seemingly dichotomous concepts was Locsin's (1995, 1998) intent, when he claimed that technological competency as a practice of nursing is an expression of caring. He claimed technological competency as caring is the practice of using nursing technologies for the purpose of "knowing" persons. This practice perspective refocuses nursing as the continuous knowing of persons through the competent use of technologies.

Technological competency as caring in nursing as a conceptual model occurs when caring and technologies in nursing coexist. The harmonization of these concepts places the practice of nursing within the context of contemporary healthcare and acknowledges their coexistence.

In explicating the relationship between technological competency and caring in nursing, a new understanding of the process of nursing must be realized. Nurses who are technological romantics (Sandelowski, 1997) do not appreciate the positive effects of technology on nursing practice. Caring is not unique *to* nursing; rather, it is unique *in* nursing (Roach, 2002). Such a statement reinforces that caring is critical to the practice of nursing.

Technological competency supports current high-tech nursing practices by validating the dependency of nursing care on technologies while enhancing its value as a practice deserving recognition for its crucial role in the management of healthcare. As a model of practice in nursing, technological competency as caring dictates ways of knowing persons as whole in the moment, a foundational belief that defines practice roles, processes, and products of the human health experience.

Nursing practice includes knowing all we can about persons. This perspective contradicts the belief that persons are predictable. For instance, being unpredictable supports the perspective that human beings, as persons, are not automatons or robots that can predictably be made to perform by flipping a switch or through computerized programming.

Appreciating the unpredictability of human beings allows the nurse to use technology to learn more about the person. The use of electrocardiographic (EKG) technology permits the nurse to know the patient's cardiac activity recorded visually in that moment, yet the nurse knows this cardiac activity will change in the next moment. A practice of nursing grounded on knowing a person's wholeness allows the nurse to understand the continuous changes that person experiences, moment to moment. In doing so, the nurse is able to appreciate the person as a living, unpredictable human being. The realization of human unpredictability negates the view of persons as objects and challenges the nurse to know the person from moment to moment. It is the recognition and appreciation of human beings as capable of experiences, as unpredictable but whole human beings complete in the moment, that makes nursing practice a legitimate and valuable healthcare practice.

> ... Being unpredictable supports the perspective that human beings, as persons, are not automatons or robots that can predictably be made to perform by flipping a switch or through computerized programming.

As a model, technological competency as caring illustrates a nursing framework guiding the practice of nursing in which technologies are continuously used to know persons as whole and complete in the moment. To be caring is to be there for the other (Paterson and Zderad, 1987). Entering the world of the other is coming to know the other as a person more fully through the competent use of technology (Locsin, 1998, 2001). Using this process, nursing becomes meaningful to the person from moment to moment.

Fallacies Regarding Caring and Technical Competency

Often, the perception of a technologically competent nurse is a person who is not caring. A traditional appreciation of a caring nurse is a person who demonstrates tender loving care, frequently expressed visually as the holding of a patient's hand. In a highly demanding technological world in which technology impacts every process of living, simply holding a patient's hand in situations that call for expertise in using technology and in interpreting high-tech responses may be the epitome of a person who is *not* caring in the moment. Being technologically competent is caring in situations of high-acuity, such as intensive care or emergency care settings. In such situations, the nurse and the patient mutually come to know each other fully. Practicing nursing using technological competency as caring permits the nurse to practice meaningfully as a caring person.

> As a model, technological competency as caring illustrates a nursing framework guiding the practice of nursing in which technologies are continuously used to know persons as whole and complete in the moment.

Nursing as a Practice Profession

Structuring knowledge advances the evolution and development of a practice profession. Scholarly inquiries using varying methodologies are crucial to this development. The appreciation of research and scholarship are critical to the development of technological competency as caring in nursing. Technological competency as caring is a fast-paced, responsive practice model involving inter- and intra-disciplinary collaboration that facilitates the evolution of knowledge and, ultimately, professional practice.

The burgeoning demands for professional nursing practice by technologically competent nurses using varying machine technologies create the need for recognizing the value of technological competency as caring as a model for practice. The practice of technological competency as caring in nursing is an illustration of the development of a theoretical model and the value of practicing nursing within a theoretical framework. As a middle-range theory, technological competency as caring fits current nursing practices because it harmonizes the seemingly dichotomous concepts of technology and caring. Technologically competent nurses are caring nurses. The use of a theoretical model driven by contemporary practice and grounded in a philosophy of caring ultimately makes nursing practice responsive and more valuable to the attainment and maintenance of human health and well-being.

What is practicing nursing as technological competency? What is the process of nursing based on the model of technological competency as caring in nursing? How does this practice demonstrate caring? The conceptual bases, the ingredients of technological competency, and the structure and process of nursing required for its practice and for its outcomes are evident in a demanding technological healthcare setting. The ingredients of technological competency include the concepts of humans as unpredictable, whole, and complete in the moment; this allows the appreciation of nursing as a discipline and a practice based on knowledge and the recognition of a process of nursing that is guided by practice. Inherent in this model are other concepts, such as an appreciation of caring and awareness that the practice demands high-tech assessments and interventions.

> Technological competency as caring is a fast-paced, responsive, practice model involving inter- and intra-disciplinary collaboration that facilitates the evolution of knowledge and, ultimately, professional practice.

References

Boykin, A., & Schoenhofer, S. (2001). *Nursing as caring: A model for transforming practice*. New York: Jones & Bartlett, National League for Nursing Press.

Fawcett, J. (1984). The metaparadigms of nursing: Present status and future refinements. *Image: Journal of Nursing Scholarship, 16*(3), 84-87.

Juergens, M. (2002). "The Octopus". Personal communication, June 2002.

Locsin, R. (1995). Machine technologies and caring in nursing. *Image: Journal of Nursing Scholarship, 26*(2), 201-203.

Locsin, R. (1998). Technological competency as expression of caring in critical care nursing. *Holistic Nursing Practice, 12*(4), 51-56.

Locsin, R. (2001). Practicing nursing: Technological competency as an expression of caring in nursing. In Locsin, R., (2001) (ed). *Advancing technology, caring, and nursing*. Westport, CT: Auburn House.

Newman, M., Sime, A., & Corcoran-Perry, S. (1991). The focus of the discipline of nursing. *Advances in Nursing Science, 14*(1), 1-6.

Paterson, J., & Zderad, P. (1987). *Humanistic nursing*. New York: National League of Nursing Press.

Roach, S. (2002). *Caring: The human mode of being*. Ottawa, Ontario: CHA Press.

Sandelowski, M. (1997). (Ir)reconcilable differences? The debate concerning nursing and technology. *Image: Journal of Nursing Scholarship, 29*(2), 169-174.

Swanson, M. (1991). Dimensions of caring interventions. *Nursing Research, 40*, 161-166.

There is a need to continue the examination of the relations between nursing and technology, not because technology is harmful—in fact it is often wonderful—but rather because total faith in technology to the exclusion of everything else is an idolatrous, dangerous, and misplaced faith.

2

CHAPTER

Understanding Technological Competence Through Philosophy of Technology and Nursing

By Alan Barnard

Technology is a primary determinant of specific culture(s) and social relations. Nurses talk about technology, develop skills and knowledge in order to apply technology, praise the qualities of the latest computer applications, and deride the demise of human contact. Nurses attend courses to learn about new equipment, work within specialist groups that are arranged in accordance with technological roles and responsibilities, work within organizational systems that are devised to maximize the application of technology, and live in a human world that is reliant on it. Nurses work in surroundings that are increasingly symbolic and virtual. For example, electronic and multimedia technologies allow for the assessment of persons in distant, inaccessible healthcare environments. Within healthcare, there is increasing integration of nanotechnology, robotics, telemetry, computerized decision-making systems, and global technology networks that support interdisciplinary collaboration, an essential element because interrelated systems require collaborative approaches to practice.

Technology has long been a focus of attention in nursing literature. Dock and Stewart (1925) identified a process of nursing practice development that was related directly to changes in medicine and technology. They claimed that nurses were beginning to specialize in various forms of therapeutics—x-ray, electrical treatment, hydrotherapy, massage, and so on. Others assisted in the new field of laboratory work in the study of metabolism. There was also a tendency to give to the nurse some of the hospital duties formerly assigned to the intern, as in the giving of anaesthetics, the keeping of records, and other clinical ward work (Dock and Stewart, 1925, p. 304).

> Nurses talk about technology, develop skills and knowledge in order to apply technology, praise the qualities of the latest computer applications, and deride the demise of human contact.

Discourse during the last century highlighted increasing tensions between assumed goals and ideals of nursing and the increasing demands directly associated with technology (Cooper, 1993; Fairman, 1998; Henderson, 1985; Locsin, 1995, 1998; McConnell, 1990;

Ray, 1987). Opinion has remained divided as to the assumed advantages and disadvantages of technological development and the changing roles and responsibilities of nurses (Barnard, 2000b; Barnard & Sandelowski, 2001; Harding, 1980; Hawthorne, 1995; Sandelowski, 2000). Even though healthcare technology and associated practices remain highly valued, future advances in nursing must concentrate on critical engagement with technology and its associated systems of logical order. Competency with technology demands that nurses are not only able to use technology safely but also engage fully with human experiences, lives, and the needs of individuals, families, groups, and society (Locsin, 1998, Ray, 1987, 2001). These central intentions of nursing demand full consideration of technology so as to ensure nursing is not understood as a purely technical profession. Full consideration means critical understanding of practice and theoretical implications and expectations.

Within this chapter, the author endeavours to advance the understanding of technological competence through highlighting the contributions of philosophy of technology and nursing toward the recognition of the legitimate response that technology created within healthcare. An investigation into the meaning of technology argues that technological competence and nursing-technology relations are complex phenomena focused on patients and patient care.

Philosophy of Technology and Nursing

Philosophy of technology and nursing is a domain of inquiry that focuses on the experiences, meaning, and implications of technology for nursing. Advances in philosophy of technology and nursing are indicative of two major occurrences: (1) technological development advancing to such an extent that it is conceived as worthy of considerable attention and (2) intellectual advances in nursing that facilitate increased critical inquiry. Philosophy of technology and nursing is a bourgeoning area of scholarship and research that focuses critical and intellectual attention on technology. Philosophy of technology is a relatively recent focus of philosophic inquiry that has developed over the past two hundred years. It is also an attempt to interpret contemporary phenomena within the light of praxes and technologies (Ferre, 1995; Ihde, 1993). It is an approach to contemporary challenges emphasizing philosophical reflection and critique of technology. Within this context, technology becomes a focal point of cultural, ethical, professional, political, human, and social significance that receives concerted and consistent reflection and debate. Thus, it is argued that it is equally important to investigate the use and design of materials and artifacts as it is to understand technology in terms of human experience and social development. Technology is interpreted as more than a material presence and/or instrumental action because technology embodies change and is significant for interpreting gender, culture, economics, politics, values, and praxis (Feenberg, 1999; Ihde, 1995; Mitcham, 1994).

Technology embodies the desire to influence the world around us. Its meaning is subject to historical and socio-cultural bias and is associated increasingly with sophisticated machinery, industrial objects, computerized or electronic automata, scientific knowledge, and technical skills. Technology has direct association with historical, scientific, philosophical, and social precepts that are embodied in the lives, culture, politics, work, language, education, knowledge, and skills. The involvement with technology brings with it more than first-order instrumental questions related to action and usage. It has associated epistemological, axiological, ontological, and ethical challenges and raises any number of second-order questions such as: Does technology influence care? What effect(s) does efficiency have on nursing practice? What is the nature of reality in clinical environments that are reliant on computer screens and healthcare monitors? And, is there technology knowledge that is specific to nursing?

Technology is an important phenomenon that is worthy of significant philosophic reflection. Such worthiness demands a sustained focus on associated epistemological questions of knowledge, both in its modern reciprocal relations to science and as a consequence of its relations to societies and groups. It brings with it evolving axiological challenges in nursing related to values and the legitimate or non-legitimate use of technological means, and it raises metaphysical concerns. For example: In what way does technology influence the understanding of reality? Nurses engage constantly in technology-to-human relations in which questions arise as to whether humans or technology are responsible for determining or manipulating human thoughts and decisions. Technology brings challenges for reflection that are associated with, for example, volition (Barnard, 2000a), the value and quality of human life (Donley, 1991; Marck, 2000), and alterations to the per-ceptions of healthcare and nursing (Sandelowski, 1998, 2002).

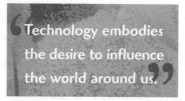

Technology embodies the desire to influence the world around us.

Philosophic inquiry can assist the response to changes that occurs reg-ularly in the practice and can assist in focusing nursing care, skills, and knowledge. For example, Pacey (1983) argued that the reduction in infant mortality in England during the 20th century was due primarily to public health reform with specific emphasis on the application of technology—improvement of water supply and sanitation and the hygienic bottling of milk. It was observed that technology is less likely to produce desired outcomes without appropriate understanding of the relations between technology and healthcare, adequate education, and enhancement of knowledge and skills. Pacey (1983) demonstrated that the outcomes of tech-nology are not understood or assessed adequately when they are interpreted as merely outcomes of the use of isolated objects, tools, and machines.

Social reforms, human relations, and ethical dilemmas confronting nurses need to be examined through philosophic inquiry. A continual and appropriate focus on technology will enable us to broaden the understand-ing of nursing practice, of human experience, of technological competence, and will help us to advance knowledge (Barnard, 1996, 1997; Barnard and Sandelowski, 2001; Fairman, 1999, 1998; Harding, 1980; Marck, 2000; Purkis, 1999; Sandelowski, 1999a).

Technology and Nursing: On the Necessity for Non-Essentialist Understanding(s) of Technology

One of the most fundamental questions to be answered in relation to phi-losophy of technology relates to the nature and meaning of technology.

Central to furthering an understanding of technology is the need to identify the meaning and nature of the phenomenon. Just as instrumental competence is not an adequate description of technological competence, the answers to the question, "what is technology?" cannot be explored adequately through limited discussions related to application and use of technologies.

Explanation and interpretation of the many and varied characteristics of technology is best for understanding technology as they highlight fundamental traits associated with the phenomenon (A. Barnard, 1999; Barnard, 2002; Fairman, 1996; Harding, 1980). Despite attempts to distill the meaning of technology into a single element, a machine for example, no one unique trait characterizes an essence that is technology. A single-trait analysis is unrewarding as a closure to understanding technology because essentialism minimizes the complexity of technology and reinforces closure. Use, for example, alternative political and social ideologies that manifest themselves in the design and the division of labor. Technology becomes standardized not in terms of a definition—because definitions merely reflect the paradigm or technological frame of the discipline area from which it originated—but in accordance with future identification and acceptance of technology. It may be the case, for example, that traditional medicines and alternative healthcare therapies and practices have suffered from a form of closure because technologies continue to be selected on the basis of dominant interests and are established as a result of cultural, sociological, and political struggles that define technological boundaries. Accepted explanation and rationalizations such as safety and technical necessity reinforce the boundaries further and force conformity with current practices. An example of this process is the ongoing struggle for the legitimacy of home-birthing practices.

> Despite attempts to distill the meaning of technology into a single element, a machine for example, no one unique trait characterizes an essence that is technology

Dominant technology and technical design reflect socio-cultural meanings and incorporate assumptions and design related to nursing practice, healthcare provision, societal values, and dominant interests. As a consequence, nurses and other groups are socialized through education and accepted practices and evidence into the technical codes of the profession. Failure to accept socialization and the code is tantamount to a failure to represent the socio-cultural meaning and political interests embedded in the profession. For example, from a social-constructivist perspective, Feenberg (1999) illustrated the process when he discussed the design characteristics of technology used for children who were factory workers during the industrial revolution. He noted that when examining photographs of technology used in factories during the time, the observer is struck by the height and general design of machinery. Technologies were designed specifically for the child labourers. Shape, specifications, and usage were determined by sociological factors that directly influenced the development of technology and the eventual development of technical codes. "Technical codes define the object in strictly technical terms in accordance with the social meaning it has acquired" (Feenberg, 1999, p. 88).

Technical codes related to nursing technologies are generally not examined or explained even though they may be gendered, relate directly to the division of labour, and possess a different professional value to technologies found commonly in other disciplines. Technical codes, socio-cultural meaning, political interests, and the fostering of efficient and rational processes are equally backgrounds or external horizons that constitute important hermeneutic dimensions of technology (Feenberg, 1999; Winner, 1986).

> "At its most obvious, technology refers to current, antiquated, and failed machinery, equipment, chemicals, and physical objects developed for use and application in nursing and healthcare."

Pills, Tubes, Drains, and Things in Their Places—These are a Few of My Favorite Things

Technology is commonly understood to be a manifestation of the orientation towards making and using tools in the world around us. It is common in nursing to focus the awareness of technology on pieces of machinery and equipment. At its most obvious, technology refers to current, antiquated, and failed machinery, equipment, chemicals, and physical objects developed for use and application in nursing and healthcare. To illustrate the point, my own work has found that the experiences of surgical nurses highlight attention to technology as machinery and equipment (Barnard & Gerber, 1999). Nurses identified technology as machinery like pulse oximeters, intravenous infusion pumps, electrocardiographs, computers, telephones, and equipment such as drugs, catheters, and dressing packs. The experience was explained by the following nurse who stated that:

> I'm just thinking now of the general ward situation and what I deal with first of all. Like the computer system, actually just entering in patient data. That's the more hands-on technology. Things like getting blood gas results or results from patients has been part of technology in a way, because it is technology that gets that information to you (Barnard, 1998, p. 125).

In this study, nurses tended to focus on technical objects that are new (modern), and they described technology as the upgrading of machinery and equipment. Technology was synonymous with innovation as noted by the following nurse who stated that technology is:

> ... equipment ... The equipment that is used and the ongoing, upgrading of the equipment that is used (Barnard, 1998, pg. 126) ... anything new. It doesn't have to be a piece of machinery; it might be a dressing ... the use of technology. Technology is the coming together of science and machinery, like the thinking of science and the substance of machinery, the actual physical pieces, be they made of metal or fabric or whatever (Barnard, 1998, p.126).

These nurses understood technology to be the tools of nursing that possess a quality of newness and are associated with scientific advancement or modern design. The understanding emphasized technology that was impressive, novel, or both. Although many nurses did identify older machinery and equipment (e.g. manual sphygmomanometer) as technology, most related a quality of newness and scientific sophistication as the reason certain machinery and equipment is considered technology.

In addition, some understood technology to be anything operated by a power source other than human (e.g. electricity). Distinctions were drawn between old and new technology on the basis of microelectronics, electricity, improved diagnostic accuracy, and efficiency. The experience was described by the following nurse who stated that technology is:

> ... equipment used to monitor patients or control apparatus, things that are attached to patients; equipment that usually requires some degree of knowledge to work them. Things attached. Things that require motors or electricity or something to keep going (Barnard, 1998, p. 127).

New or modern technology was experienced as a demonstration of the progress of nursing and healthcare and is manifest as the removal of the nurse as the principle agent responsible for ongoing technological activity. The perception was that modern technology is essentially independent from the efforts of any nurse. It could operate independently and had, seemingly, an intelligence of its own. The technology of the modern surgical ward is electronic, impressive, quick, and innovative. The experience was explained by the following nurse who stated that technology is:

> (Nurse) ... pumps, the IV drips, that's all a system; catheters, irrigations, central lines are technology. There are a million things. It might be thermometers, the new thermometers. (Interviewer) Why do you say new thermometers? (Nurse) Oh, and the old thermometers, but I'm thinking of modern, in today's terms now. (Interviewer) So the old one is as much technology? (Nurse) Yes, that's just the development of technology.

The more modern version of technology would be the electrical ones (Barnard, 1998, p. 127)

Finally, for some nurses the development of electronics and diagnostic sophistication influenced their understanding of the phenomenon to such an extent that older machinery and equipment were no longer described as technology. The experience is highlighted in the following conversation between the interviewer and the nurse who stated that technology is:

> *(Nurse)* ... something that you can do manually but has a machine or a component with electricity supplied to it. ... like the manual blood pressure cuff and the dynamap, and so you're relying on something other than what you are. So you are relying on electricity to come into the machine for it to work and you can't manually override that, you can't just say I will do it manually; I would consider that technology in my frame of reference. But I guess that if you didn't have a sphygmomanometer, and you got a sphygmomanometer then you'd probably call that technology. So I wonder if it's not time related. *(Interviewer)* What do you mean by time related? *(Nurse)* If you are a graduate [nurse] today, you're probably very familiar with thermometers that are membrane thermometers gauging the temperature. To me that would be technology but because it's their beginning point, they may not see it as technology. They may see what comes after that as being technology, which may be a further development of technology. Does that make sense? So in the case of the sphygmomanometer, the sphygmomanometer that I know that I have to pump up, and is a free standing thing, to me isn't technology, but the complexity of the machine with electricity and everything else is technology (Barnard, 1998, p. 128)

Thus the qualities of newness and electronic sophistication combine to define the meaning of technology. In the above example, the nurses' experience was so discrete that older machinery and equipment were no longer acknowledged as technology. Innovation and advanced design were the reasons why machinery and equipment were accepted as technology. For some nurses, modern and sophisticated objects that are powered by an external power source are more technological than older manually operated means that are readily available. It is apparent that many of the tools of nursing are seemingly so familiar and ready-to-hand that they are less identified as technology for their link with daily activities, practices, actions, and roles.

Is Technology Just Machinery and Equipment?

Even though machinery and equipment frequently are the focus of professional (and societal) attention, the tendency to focus on them singularly is surprising given the diversity of technology and the practical nature of nursing. Further, it is reasonable to expect that a lot of investigation has occurred into the origin, history, form, and significance of nursing technology. However, little has been done to investigate the relations between technology and nursing (Barnard & Cushing, 2001; Fairman, 1998; Locsin, 2001; Sandelowski, 2000) or to identify subtle distinctions between types of technologies or the way specific technologies have developed and influenced nursing practices. The technologies of nursing have not been examined adequately. Much attention has been given to debating the qualities of machinery and equipment as either paragons or metaphors for the future hope of nursing or the future conflict of nursing (Barnard, 1996, 2000b; Sandelowski, 1997, 2000).

Thus a lot of nursing technology is not visible (i.e. lacks recognition as technology specific to nursing), and it is therefore instructive to draw upon the work of authors such as Mitcham (1994) who notes that technological artifacts can be explained and catalogued as different types. The types are not mutually exclusive; they call forth a unique history and analysis and yet they describe technology that is lived with, operated, or set in motion. Based on Mitcham's catalogue, it can be claimed that there are eight different types of nursing technologies: *clothes* (e.g. shroud, pajamas); *utensils* (e.g. bed pan, kidney dish); *structures* (e.g. hospital ward, isolation room); *apparatus* (e.g. sluice); *utilities* (e.g. gas, electrical power); *tools* (e.g. wheel chair, catheter, sphygmomanometer); *machines* (e.g. intravenous infusion pump); and *automata* (e.g. blood warmer, refrigerator, computer). In addition, there remain three other types that could be included as nursing technologies depending on their context, use, and interpretation: *tools of doing* (e.g. nurse's watch), *objects of art or religion* (e.g. nurse's uniform), and toys (e.g. board games, therapeutic equipment).

The catalogue of types not only embraces technologies associated with modern electronics, diagnostics, and treatments, but also fully represents even the most commonplace and ordinary technologies of nursing. It confirms the intensely technological nature of nursing and the diverse range of phenomena that come together to constitute many aspects of nursing practice.

Knowledge, Skill, and Action

Even though nursing is a practical occupation and knowledge is expressed most often through the way nurses perform their work, practical significance can understate characteristics of technology that are expressed less clearly as practical performance. Technology not only encompasses new and old machinery, automata, utensils, and so on, but also the development of skills and knowledge within the context of efficient and effective political, economic, human, and administrative structures (Allan, 1988; Barnard, 2002; Barnard & Sandelowski, 2001; Fairman, 1996; Harding, 1980; Pelletier, 1989).

Nursing has witnessed a steady association with numerous new roles and responsibilities as a result of specialization and changes to the division of labor (e.g. as a result of developing medical roles and responsibilities) (Sandelowski, 1999b, 2000), and a societal environment in which scientific and technological advancement is increasing and expected to continue to increase. As nurses have become increasingly involved with more and varied technologies, so too has there been a need to foster greater knowledge and skills. Thus, the meaning of technology must be expressed also in relation to knowledge and skills associated with, for example, technology application, repair (troubleshooting), design, and assessment. It is essential in many clinical environments that nurses demonstrate competency in skills and knowledge associated with the application of specific advanced technologies and demonstrate an ability to operate within advanced systems of information production and retrieval. For example, it is by way of computerization and the use of formal and efficient technologies (e.g., screens and network communications), that increasingly comprehensive organizational processes, procedures, and inter-relations between different fields and subfields of healthcare are integrated. Without appropriate knowledge and skills, a technology has limited meaning or use and a practitioner may be inefficient and potentially unsafe. Technological competence demands significant attention to knowledge and skill development.

> The real aspect of technological development within post-industrial society is the development of technique.

Technique

Fundamental to technological development is the establishment of human, political, and economic arrangements that ensure the efficient use and application of technology. Technology cannot be understood adequately as mere methodology or a collection of artifacts and objects. Increasing systems of human, political, and economic control are features of modern technology. It is an historical past that emphasized primary consideration of energy transforming machines such as steam engines and airplanes. Analyses and discourse have argued that the new and real emphasis of technology is now procedural (Borgmann, 1984; Ellul, 1964, 1972, 1980; Mitcham, 1994; Pacey, 1983, 1999; Postman, 1992). That is, how nurses *do* things, the systems that organize production, and the efforts they make for the sake of efficiency. The real aspect of technological development within post-industrial society is the development of technique. That is, the establishment of a growing system of efficient and logical order. Technique is the creation of the kind of thinking that is necessary for technology to develop and be applied in an efficient and rational manner. Failure to work within a system means potential inefficient and ineffective control of technology and outcomes. Obvious examples of technique include economic rationalism, protocols, communication skills, efficiency drives, diagnostic-related groups, and time-and-motion studies.

25

Technique is not an entity or specific thing in and of itself. Technique is a mentality that operates within societies that determines behaviors, thinking, and intentionality. It seeks to control individual differences; predetermine causal relations; emphasize specialization of practice; enhance conformity; and bring sameness to product, processes, and thought. It is an attitude and a way of life. It is what Winner (1977) refers to as the gestalt of the modern man and woman.

Technique emphasizes primacy of reason as the governing priority of human activity and as a tool by which people attempt to control the internal, passionate, and emotional world of everyday life—in addition to the more controllable external world. Reason is interpreted as the analytic organ of the mind (Temple, 1980, p. 225) through which nurses attempt to:

> ...order and organize; make divisions of experience into concrete observations; distinguish among observations; delineate patterns and relationships among discrete facts; relate means to ends; see options; make inferences, deductions, and comparisons; assess internal coherences and make projections from them.

> 66 ... The most easily discernable and obvious form of efficiency is the machine because it seeks to mechanize work in such a fashion as to bring all the various parts together in order to obtain desired outcomes and reduce the possibility of human error, chance, or difference. 99

Temple (1980) explains that Ellul (1964), exposed technique as a complex phenomenon that is constituted of three subtle yet important aspects. First, technique adheres to a primacy of reason to govern practical realms. Second, it requires a desire for efficiency as a further faculty in order to assist its purposes and to justify its activity. In everyday life, the practice of increasing efficiency is akin to the manager who seeks to streamline methods and actions in order to obtain certain outcomes. Ellul (1964) explains that the most easily discernable and obvious form of efficiency is the machine because it seeks to mechanize work in such a fashion as to bring all the various parts together in order to obtain desired outcomes and reduce the possibility of human error, chance, or difference. Ellul's notion of efficiency is concerned with practical utility, guaranteeing results, reducing waste, and the construction of systems that simplify and systematize previously uncontrolled or random activity. The desire to maximize efficiency in practice through the refinement of action has continued to be a cornerstone to best practices. Importantly, the multiplication of efficient practices does not in itself constitute a problem. The specific problem occurs when quantitative changes come into direct conflict with the qualitative needs, experiences, goals, values, and so on, of individuals, practitioners, families, and cultures.

There is nothing dangerous per se about efficiency as an intended goal, and the desire for inefficiency is not an appropriate outcome. Further to this, there is nothing new about order and efficiency as reasonable and worthwhile goals. They have both guided invention and activities through human history. However there is a third dimension to technique that brings it into a new realm of relations and highlights it as both a modern phenomenon and a challenge for every nurse.

> There is nothing dangerous per se about efficiency as an intended goal, and the desire for inefficiency is not an appropriate outcome.

The third dimension to technique highlights the spread of the principle of efficiency and rational order into *every realm of human activity and thinking* (Ellul, 1964). Technical reasoning has become so prevalent in society, organizations, and activities that people are increasingly incapable of thinking outside its boundaries in their search for meaning. There comes a point where individuals, organizations, and practitioners find it almost impossible to see other ways to organize the world apart from efficient reason or rationality. Technique is the creation of economic, human, and political systems that brings us increasingly into line with technology (means) and imparts control over increasingly varied human and non-human aspects of the world. It reduces the thinking and what should be intensely human-centric activities such as nursing to measurable and predictable processes.

Technique is increasingly the standard by which social relations, activities, organizations, humans, and political activity are constituted and judged appropriate. A material and symbolic world of order is being created for directing the way nurses live their lives. It has specific intrinsic characteristics and brings about specific results that derive from its extrinsic relationships with other structures of society (Ellul, 1964, 1980; Temple, 1980). The importance of technique for nursing, healthcare, and society should not be underestimated. Our embracing technique is the biggest gamble. Technique structures collective behaviour and influences individual lives and professional perspectives. It is a characteristic of technological society that emphasizes a kind of technical thinking that organizes and arranges everything in accordance with technology. Technique is a phenomenon that has been explored in numerous philosophies of technology (Borgmann, 1984; Ellul, 1964; Feenberg, 1999; Ferre, 1995; Ihde, 1993; Mitcham, 1994; Winner, 1977) and is bound inextricably to technology as a major determinant of healthcare practices, nursing, and modern life. According to Lovekin (1991), "technique is a mentality, a system, a way of culture and society, and a way of life. Technique is metaphysics; a manifestation of the ultimately real; an addiction; and an obsession that nurses wish to do nothing about." (p. 65)

> Anyone with a commitment to technological competence needs, where appropriate, to be affronted by the ways technique can manifest in practice.

Thus, to a technical mind, a woman birthing is a body in need of control; breast-feeding is a support group in need of formation; home birth is an uncontrolled risk to be educated against; natural childbirth is the design and establishment of a birthing room; and nursing and midwifery practices are a technical phenomenon to be directed by technology, objective outcomes, predefined protocols, and clearly defined policies. Differences between tradition, culture, ethical values, artistic expression, and behaviours are reduced to either demonstratable schemata, policies, human activity, organizational management, and educational goals or are marginalized because they are not open to efficient ordering or measurement.

The Challenge of Technique for Technological Competence

Efficiency and rational order in every realm of nursing practice is a significant framework and is a hermeneutic dimension of healthcare (Feenberg, 1999; Mitcham, 1994). Anyone with a commitment to technological competence needs, where appropriate, to be affronted by the ways technique can manifest in practice. Technique marginalizes the incorporation of subjective and non-technical phenomenon (e.g. human experience) by either negating its importance or framing it within rational and organized order. According to Mitcham (1994), the primary challenge it presents to us all is that it resists incorporation into or subordination to non-technical attitudes and ways of thinking. It explains other actions as forms of itself and thereby transforms them into itself. It constitutes, as it were, the social manifestation of Heidegger's gestalt (p. 59).

Yet nurses expect the world nurses live in to be devised in accordance with technique. Adaptation to technique is spontaneous. After all, technique is the natural context of the modern person! The healthcare context constitutes a tangible and increasingly real, universal combination of technologies and practices that operate within environments to which most people and families are well prepared and adapted. The urban environment and the modern hospital are the real world. Natural events (e.g. unmediated events and practices) occur only on an accidental or secondary basis because policies and protocols are increasingly expected. Accordingly, healthcare occurs within a pre-determined rhythm based on the efficient application of resources, policies, plans, and the division of labor.

The participating midwife/nurse/patient/doctor/woman/man gain the pleasure of being part of a technological healthcare system, reassured by the predictable nature of its organization, control, and efficiency. However, if participation is not desired or appropriate, or if the incorporation of the subjective and non-technical is valued, as in the desire to provide holistic and individualized care, then there will be feelings that practice is excessively standardized. Care can be perceived as secondary to the efficient goals of hospitals, practitioners, and healthcare managers, particularly given that many aspects of nursing practice are hidden and are less obvious as a result of their subjective nature and human-relations focus (e.g. spending time with a person experiencing significant emotional distress).

> **Care can be perceived as secondary to the efficient goals of hospitals, practitioners, and healthcare managers, particularly given that many aspects of nursing practice are hidden and are less obvious as a result of their subjective nature and human-relations focus.**

Ellul (1964) highlights four important features of technique. The features are critical for understanding modern nursing and highlight the challenges that are before each nurse, the profession, and healthcare.

First, technique is the sum-total of an ensemble of means, rationally arrived at in order to obtain greatest efficiency in every realm of practice. It is a commonplace mentality and an intentionality that is lived out in society. Technique is the basis for a world that is being constructed in the shell of the old. It is the new *natural* milieu. A milieu characterized by increasing technological order governed by efficiency and rationalization. Nurses practice in environments and live in societies where technique increasingly constitutes the real (natural) world. Healthcare practices based on non-rationalized and spontaneous action are increasingly an accidental or random addition to the rational order that has been established for the efficient facilitation of nursing and medicine.

Second, there has emerged a type of technological consciousness that is based on increasing rationality. To this end, nurses are moving increasingly away from a consciousness that is based on the use of tools as extensions of the body to a consciousness where no such extension is required. The electronic sphygmomanometer, the electronic fetal monitor, and the digital read-out thermometer are all part of a new commonplace consciousness.

Third, human, technical, political, and economic technique is the basis for healthcare delivery. The systematic nature of the relations created encourages embracement of technique as a way of life and a way of practicing nursing.

Fourth, the order that is created by technique and the integration of technical phenomenon into the world has become a sacred order in which further system relations can and do evolve and criticism is rare. Technique seeks nothing other than to replicate itself. The sacred order created has an associated aura of mystery that may in fact be perceived as awe-inspiring in its effects and promises. Ellul (1975) argues that technique is a veritable general topography of the world that encompasses actions, space, contexts, material, spiritual, the transcendent, and everything close at hand. Under these conditions, the profession of nursing is at risk of becoming nothing more than technique in and of itself. That is, nursing is perceived as increasingly meaningless unless it is informed by a manual, a policy, or a handbook that informs us of the *one best way* to do it.

> Under these conditions, the profession of nursing is at risk of becoming nothing more than technique in and of itself.

Radical Nursing

And what do nurses do about technique as nurses strive for technological competence? Moore (1998) notes that the outcome of the development of technique has not been oppression but submission to a hope in a greater good—submission to a kind of machine-ness in the thinking and acting. Technique demands devotion to its agenda and has enveloped us within networks of material, conceptual, and technological possibilities that transform healthcare and the practice of nursing. Nurses are obliged to take account of every human, economic, and political problem as a matter of policy and planning, yet believe themselves to be free to provide individualized and holistic care. Addressing the challenge of technique demands a great effort on the part of each nurse. Suggestions are made in this chapter for addressing technique. The suggestions, however, do not emphasize adequately the enormity of the problem and the challenges each person will face.

> The first move towards freedom from technique is appropriate recognition of the problem.

The first move towards freedom from technique is appropriate recognition of the problem. Central to meaningfully engaging with the human condition and the establishment of a consciousness related to technological competence is recognition that nurses are not often free to go about their activities and make decisions and choices. Nurses do so within guidelines, systems, and policy. Second, nurses need, where appropriate, to dispel the idea that nurses must control every human activity. Nurses need to seriously ask themselves what gives meaning to their lives, the profession, and what are the desires and needs of each person to whom nurses provide care. Once this is understood, nurses need to foster a certain detachment of the importance of technique and develop a renewed respect for human experience and the sanctity of human life. Nurses must be willing at every stage to be certain of the reasons why they do things, the necessity and appropriateness of choices that are made, the suitability of care provided, and the necessity to seek out something different where necessary. Third, there is need for a concerted effort to reflect upon nursing care and the importance of genuinely determining care that not only addresses the needs of institutions but the needs and requirements of individuals and families. Finally, nurses need to engage in discussion with every person about the impact of technique and seek to influence where possible organizations and decision makers.

> Professional advancement in association with technology is appropriate, but advancement must include active participation in seeking to optimize both healthcare intervention and understanding.

Summary

In this chapter, philosophy of technology has been identified as an important developing area for nursing, and a complex interpretation of technology has been outlined that emphasizes technology and its relations to the context of modern nursing and healthcare. There are many issues related to technology that need to be addressed by nurses, and there are a number of key areas that need attention in relation to philosophy of technology and nursing.

- Nurses need to interpret technology from a range of non-essentialist perspectives.

- Nurses need specific and refined analyses of technology that rely less on commonplace generalizations about, for example, dehumanization or uncritical celebration of unsubstantiated advantages of technology, than on considered critical reflection on discrete interventions and technologies.

- Philosophy of technology encourages us to reflect on technology from perspectives that are wider than the relation between technology and instrumental action. For example, many countries do not experience the same levels of techno-scientific development in healthcare services and nursing practices, yet they are increasingly influenced by technique.

- What are the implications of increasing technology on nursing in developing countries in terms of future practice, management, and education?

- What lessons can be learned from contemporary nursing practices that are instructive for healthcare provision and knowledge development?

- What is or could be the future for technology and nursing? Ihde (1993) notes that the integration of philosophy in applied ethics contexts such as nursing, medicine, and healthcare comes too late. Theorists and philosophers are required to fix up and inquire into changes and developments that have already occurred in practice. Ihde (1993) notes that better assistance could be provided by philosophy through its inclusion in development processes. Professional advancement in association with technology is appropriate, but advancement must include active participation in seeking to optimize both healthcare intervention and understanding. The challenge is commonplace to society and nursing and was identified by Ellul (1997, pg. 41) who noted that:

> People will ask, then, is a pure intellectual work what is needed? In a certain measure, yes. And it seems to me quite vain to want to dispense with intelligence in order to direct the action and to want to act right away and at any price, without knowing what one is going to do, without previously having sat down to count the cost. Now this is very characteristic of the utopia and of technical solutions: One applies no serious intellectual method and one seeks immediately to govern the action.

There is a need to continue the examination of the relations between nursing and technology, not because technology is harmful—in fact it is often wonderful—but rather because total faith in technology to the exclusion of everything else is an idolatrous, dangerous, and misplaced faith. The quantity of technological change guarantees nothing as to its quality. Nurses need to embrace a healthy and radical ambivalence towards technology with particular reference to technique. Responsibility for the future of nursing and healthcare involves more than learning to use machinery and equipment, and it involves more than the allowance of a momentum in which acceptance of change is a logical aspiration.

Although Ihde (1993) highlights that philosophy of technology can lead to changes in practice by informing practitioners of ways to understand and respond to challenges and dilemmas, Mitcham (1994) notes it is not clear how philosophy of technology contributes to immediate decision making that is undertaken under pressure. However, the need for decisiveness should not be confused with decisiveness about needs.

Philosophical and theoretical interpretation of technology and nursing is emerging at a timely period and offers opportunities to enrich the insight into questions and challenges related to the nature and scope of technology and nursing (Barnard, 2002). It will provide avenues for the development of a consciousness specific to nursing and has the potential to improve care that seeks appropriate use of technology. There is opportunity for us to make a profound contribution to healthcare through a focus on the relations between technology, technological competence, technique, nursing, and the health of people.

References

Allan, J.D., Hall, B.A. (1988). Challenging the focus on technology: a critique of the medical model in a changing healthcare system. *Advances in Nursing Science, 10*, 22-34.

Barnard, A. (1996). Technology and nursing: An anatomy of definition. *International Journal of Nursing Studies, 33*, 433-441.

Barnard, A. (1997). A critical review of the belief the technology is a neutral object and nurses are its master. *Journal of Advanced Nursing, 26*, 126-131.

Barnard, A. (1998). *Understanding technology in contemporary surgical nursing: A phenomenographic examination.* Unpublished doctoral thesis, The University of New England, Armidale, Australia.

Barnard, A. (1999). Nursing and the primacy of technological progress. *International Journal of Nursing Studies, 36,* 435-442.

Barnard, A. (2000a). Alteration to will as an experience of technology and nursing. *Journal of Advanced Nursing, 31*(5), 1136-1144.

Barnard, A. (2000b). Technology and the Australian nursing experience. In J. Daly, S. Speedy, & D. Jackson (Eds.), *Contexts of nursing: An introduction* (pp. 163-176). Sydney, Australia: Maclennan & Petty.

Barnard, A. (2002). Philosophy of technology and nursing. *Nursing Philosophy, 3,* 15-26.

Barnard, A., & Cushing, A. (2001). Technology and historical inquiry in nursing. In R. Locsin (Ed.), *Advancing Technology, Caring and Nursing* (pp. 12-21). Westport, CT: Auburn House.

Barnard, A., & Gerber, R. (1999). Understanding technology in contemporary surgical nursing: A phenomenographic examination. *Nursing Inquiry, 6,* 157-170.

Barnard, A., & Sandelowski, M. (2001). Technology and humane nursing care: (Ir)reconcilable or invented difference? *Journal of Advanced Nursing, 34,* 367-375.

Borgmann, A. (1984). *Technology and the character of contemporary life.* Chicago: Chicago University Press.

Cooper, M.C. (1993). The intersection of technology and care in the ICU. *Advances in Nursing Science, 15*(3), 23-32.

Dock, L., & Stewart, I. (1925). *A short history of nursing.* New York: Putman.

Donley, R. (1991). Spiritual dimensions of healthcare: Nursing mission. *Nursing & Healthcare, 12,* 178-183.

Ellul, J. (1964). *The technological society.* New York: Alfred A. Knopf.

Ellul, J. (1972). The Technological order. In C. Mitcham & R. Mackey (Eds.), *Philosophy and technology* (pp. 86-105). New York: The Free Press.

Ellul, J. (1975). *The new demons* (E.C. Hopkins, Trans.). New York: Seabury.

Ellul, J. (1980). *The technological system.* New York: Continuum.

Ellul, J. (1997). Needed: A new Karl Marx! In, *Sources and trajectories* (pp. 29-48). Grand Rapids, MI: William B. Eerdmanns.

Fairman, J. (1996). Response to tools of the trade: Analysing technology as object in nursing. *Scholarly Inquiry for Nursing Practice: An International Journal, 10,* 17-21.

Fairman, J., & D'Antonio, P. (1999). Virtual power: Gendering the nurse-technology relationship. *Nursing Inquiry, 6,* 178-186.

Fairman, J., & Lynaugh, J.E. (1998). *Critical care nursing: A history.* Philadelphia: The University of Pennsylvania Press.

Feenberg, A. (1999). *Questioning technology.* New York: Routledge.

Ferre, F. (1995). *Philosophy of technology.* London: The University of Georgia Press.

Harding, S. (1980). Value laden technologies and the politics of nursing. In S.F. Spicker & S. Gadow (Ed.), *Nursing: Images and ideals* (pp. 49-75). New York: Springer.

Hawthorne, D.L., & Yurkovich, N.J. (1995). Science, technology, caring and the professions: Are they compatible? *Journal of Advanced Nursing, 21,* 1087-1091.

Henderson, V. (1985). The essence of nursing in high technology. *Nursing Administration Quarterly, 9*(4), 1-9.

Ihde, D. (1993). *Philosophy of technology: an introduction.* Bloomington, IN: Indiana University Press.

Ihde, D. (1995). Philosophy of technology, 1975-1995. *Techne, 1,* 1-6.

Locsin, R. (1995). Machine technologies and caring in nursing. *Image: Journal of Nursing Scholarship, 27*(3), 201-203.

Locsin, R. (1998). Technologic competence as caring in critical care. *Holistic Nursing Practice, 12,* 50-56.

Locsin, R. (2001). *Advancing technology, Nursing and caring.* Westport, CT: Auburn House.

Lovekin, D. (1991). *Technique, discourse and consciousness: An introduction to the philosophy of Jacques Ellul.* Madison, NJ: Associated University Press.

Marck, P.B. (2000). Recovering ethics after 'technics:' Developing critical text on technology. *Nursing Ethics, 7,* 5-14.

McConnell, E.A. (1990). The impact of machines on the work of critical care nurses. *Critical Care Nursing Quarterly, 12*(4), 45-52.

Mitcham, C. (1994). Thinking through technology: The path between engineering and philosophy. Chicago: The University of Chicago Press.

Moore, R.C. (1998). Hegemony, agency, and dialectical tensions in Ellul's technological society. *Journal of Communication, 48*(3), 129-144.

Pacey, A. (1983). *The culture of technology.* Cambridge, MA: MIT Press.

Pacey, A. (1999). *Meaning in technology.* Cambridge, MA: The MIT Press.

Pelletier, D. (1989). Healthcare technology: Sharpening the definition and establishing aspects of the social context. *Australian Health Review, 12*(3), 56-64.

Postman, N. (1992). Technology: The surrender of culture to technology. New York: Alfred A. Knopf.

Purkis, M.E. (1999). Embracing technology: An exploration of the effects of writing nursing. *Nursing Inquiry, 6*, 147-156.

Ray, M.A. (1987). Technological caring: A new model in critical care. *Dimensions of Critical Care Nursing, 6*, 166-173.

Ray, M.A. (2001). Complex culture and technology: Toward a global caring communitarian ethics of nursing. In R. Locsin (Ed.), *Advancing technology, Caring, and Nursing* (pp. 41-52). Westport, CT: Auburn House.

Sandelowski, M. (1997). (Ir)reconcilable differences? The debate concerning nursing and technology. *Image: Journal of Nursing Scholarship, 29*(2), 169-174.

Sandelowski, M. (1998). Looking to care or caring to look? Technology and the rise of spectacular nursing. *Holistic Nursing Practice, 12*(4), 1-11.

Sandelowski, M. (1999a). Culture, conceptive technology, and nursing. *International Journal of Nursing Studies, 36*, 13-20.

Sandelowski, M. (1999b). Venous envy: The post-World War II debate over IV nursing. *Advances in Nursing Science, 22*(1), 52-62.

Sandelowski, M. (2000). *Devices and desires: Gender, technology and American nursing.* Chapel Hill, NC: The University of North Carolina.

Sandelowski, M. (2002). Visible humans, vanishing bodies, and virtual nursing: Complications of life, presence, place, and identity. *Advances in Nursing Science, 24*(3), 58-70.

Temple, K. (1980). The sociology of Jacques Ellul. *Research in Philosophy of Technology, 3,* 223-261.

Winner, L. (1977). *Autonomous technology.* Cambridge, MA: The MIT Press.

Winner, L. (1986). *The whale and the reactor.* Chicago: University of Chicago Press.

CHAPTER 3

Inside a Trojan Horse: Technology, Intentionality & Metaparadigms of Nursing

By Marguerite J. Purnell

Once Upon a Myth

At a wedding feast of the gods, Aphrodite gave Paris, the son of the king of Troy, the most beautiful woman in the world—Helen, wife of Menelaus. Paris went to Sparta to claim his prize and was treated as a royal guest by the unsuspecting Menelaus. Instead of repaying Menelaus' kindness, Paris abducted Helen and took her to Troy to be his wife.

Menelaus was outraged. All of Greece took up arms and laid siege to Troy. For ten long years the Greeks were unable to break down the Trojan city walls. However, Odysseus, who was known for his cleverness and cunning, ordered a large, hollow wooden horse to be built by the artist Epeius. Odysseus and a cadre of Greek warriors climbed inside and waited outside the city gates while the rest of the Greek fleet sailed away.

The Trojans rejoiced and marveled at the artistic creation. Ignoring the counsel of two wise men, the Trojans drew the gift horse inside the city gates and began celebrating their victory over the Greeks. In the night, when the city was asleep, Odysseus and his warriors crept out of the horse, slaughtered the king, and burned down the city. Troy was overtaken by a ruse.

From Myth to Metaphor

As both metaphor and allegory, this story is rich with meaning and implications. Exotic philosophy, art, and technology are united in a gift horse that few can refuse. Stealth, surprise, and irreversibility mark the panoply of technological dominion that is unleashed within the gates. The intention of the creators is fulfilled: The Trojan horse is changed from wondrous gift to relentless conqueror.

In this era of remarkable change, the call to contemporary nursing is, without doubt, a call to practice in a technologically mediated profession. Western medicine is burgeoning with innovation and change that is spearheaded by advances in biomedical technology. As the interface between medicine, medical technology, and the patient, nurses fluidly inhabit and unite both worlds within a person-centered practice. The lines between technology introduced in nursing and technology experienced in the routine of everyday life are rapidly becoming blurred and even indefinable. Technology is a mercurial shape-shifter and surreal dimension-dancer. As soon as it begins to be described and defined, technology transforms, and descriptions are rendered outdated and moot, relegated to history in the face of the greater implications of "next generation" technology. Transcending the notion of keeping pace with technological change invites a discourse not only of trajectory, or cause and effect, or strange attraction, or utility, but of ontological and epistemological significance that lays siege to our understanding of who we are as human beings, and more particularly, as nurses.

> "Technology is a mercurial shape-shifter and surreal dimension-dancer. As soon as it begins to be described and defined, technology transforms, and descriptions are rendered outdated and moot, relegated to history in the face of the greater implications of "next generation" technology."

The problems that beset nurse scholars in addressing the advent of sophisticated biomedical technology are evidenced in the the multitude of their writings (Barnard, 1999; Cooper, 1993; Locsin, 1995; McConnell, 1998, Purnell, 1998; Ray, 1987; Sandelowski, 1997; Walters, 1995) that seek to divide the myth of technology from the reality of technology. In article upon article, scholars critically examine the relationship of the human nurse with nonhuman technology, diverting energy and focus away from advancing knowledge about the relationship between nurse and patient. The unprecedented scrutiny of technology and of its influence on the nurse flies in the face of what were formerly considered priorities for research—the patient and the nurse-patient relationship. The question can reasonably be asked, however, that if the nurse is the mediator between the biotechnology and the one nursed, then the study of the relationship between nurse and biotechnology is not only warranted, but justified. Such a focus on technology and the nurse has not been reflected in the meta-paradigm of nursing, those clusters of loosely agreed-upon concepts that nursing inhabits and that inhabit nursing. Neither the nurse, nor technology, nor the nurse *and* technology are included as domain concepts among the generally accepted paradigm concepts of the discipline of nursing.

> In searching for reasons to account for the invisibility of the contribution of nurses, the twin legacies of inherited social inequities and the devaluation of females do not reflect a major contribution to the problem: Nurses themselves had not placed a premium on who they were and on their unique contribution to human welfare.

Omission of the Nurse as Domain Concept

The reasons for the exclusion of the nurse as a domain concept are steeped in tradition and in the birth-pangs of nursing as a discipline and profession. With the post World War II growth of academic nursing in the 1950s, researchers focused on development of clinical knowledge to improve outcomes of care and on enhancing the nurse-patient relationship in the provision of care. In searching for reasons to account for the invisibility of the contribution of nurses, the twin legacies of inherited social inequities and the devaluation of females do not reflect a major contribution to the problem: Nurses *themselves* had not placed a premium on who they were and on their unique contribution to human welfare.

Historical sketches in nursing research textbooks record that nurses studied themselves for a period of time in the 1960s and 1970s—more than thirty years ago. When nursing was attempting to validate its self-election as a discipline and profession and as a science by the National Academy of

Sciences in 1977 (Pressler & Fitzpatrick, 1988), mature research method-ologies were borrowed from other disciplines, such as sociology, in the absence of tested research methodologies in nursing (Azjen, 1985). This initial examination of nurses and on defining their practice surrendered to the overriding importance of studying patient outcomes of nursing. Recognized as having the greater need for the focus of nursing research, research conducted on the patient was also a conduit for obtaining scarce gov-ernment research funding. Accordingly, research on the patient acquired increased importance, in tandem with the ability of nurses to acquire larger research grants.

> *Familiarity with the idea of who the nurse is and with the osten-sible role of the nurse is grounded in history.*

Funding for research on nurses has been spurred by the current unprecedented cyclical depletion of nurses in practice and the increasing consternation of healthcare institutions globally at their inability to attract and retain nurses and to remain financially viable (Purnell, Horner, & Westman, 2001). Funding, including federal, state, local, and private, is being channelled into the study of the recruitment and retention of nurses. Yet despite the attention of government, healthcare institutions, nurse edu-cation institutions, and of society, mention of the nurse as a subject for study in tandem with other aspects of the metaparadigm continues to engender among nurses an almost knee-jerk, exclusionary reaction to the idea. Clearly, hindsight and greater nursing knowledge about the nurse-patient relationship illuminates the need for a balanced approach in which the person and health of the nurse is valued and esteemed as well as the per-son and health of the one nursed.

Technology as Domain Concept: A New Paradigm?

The reason for the non-inclusion of technology in the metaparadigm is more complex. Familiarity with the idea of who the nurse is and with the ostensible role of the nurse is grounded in history. Familiarity with the idea of technology, on the other hand, is grounded in the idea of uncertainty and immense change, both substantively and conceptually. In 19th and 20th century society, technology was popularly conceived of in terms of immense blocks of machinery, engines, huge tools, and mass production with the attendant de-skilling of craftsmen. Technology was a behemoth that could produce more, in less time, with less effort, and with less human labor. The transition to the computer age in the mid 19th century began an inexorable advance to complexity that has been like none other in human record. Fit, form, function, and power have since been reconceptualized away from the gigantic to the propagation of micro- and nano-technologies. Bigger is now *not* better: This dramatic change, occurring within decades, may be understood in terms of 20th century spacecraft—sleek symbols of technological power and might that were sent forth into the cosmos of outer space. In the 21st century, the opposite holds true where nanotechnology is measured in billionths of a meter and where instruments are being built, sized, and operated on a scale of less than 100 nanometers (100 billionths of a meter) or the size of a virus. Nanometer-scaled medical robots carrying antiviral or antibiotic payloads and able to assemble and reconstruct human tissue, will be vectored into the human cosmos of inner-space within a few decades (Weber, 2002).

Considering Technology and Nursing

In considering the entry and acceptance of technology in nursing, we are called to earnestly inquire "What is it? Why is it?" and "How is it?" in relation to ourselves as human beings, to nursing as a discipline of knowledge, and through this knowledge to the invigoration of the practice of nursing. Into all these areas, including human beings themselves, technology now permanently resides by virtue of its existence as an inseparable, grafted-in aspect of our bodies and of our lives. Acknowledgement of this irrevocable tenancy in nursing is overtly discussed in current nursing literature and routinely included as part of the vision of nursing. The Honor Society of Nursing, Sigma Theta Tau International, for example, includes as part of its vision and mission statement: "A vision to lead: To create a global community of nurses who lead in using nursing scholarship, knowledge, and technology to improve the health of the world's people" (Sigma Theta Tau International, 2003).

The question must be asked that if theories are grounded in the belief systems of the nursing paradigm, and if conceptual definitions of theories are congruent with the beliefs set forth in the paradigm, then why are contemporary theories of nursing that encompass the relationship between nurse and technology as a central focus of concern not reflected in metaparadigm concepts? In order to answer this question, we ask further: Is technology an essential domain of nursing? If so, to what technology do we refer?

The answers to these questions may lie in the nature of technology itself. In the healthcare industry—and by extension in nursing in technological or medically ordered settings—biomedical technology holds dominion. Technology in nursing is commonly conceived of as an object in the form of such machines as computers, monitors, and instruments of evaluation and diagnosis.

However, the advancement of medical technology has rendered such a conception as elementary. In particular, biomedical technology has advanced beyond the external environment, beyond the stage of crudely interpolated intracorporeal part or device, such as the artificial heart in the 1960s, to the stage of total integration with the human body such as the sophisticated embedding of the technology of artificially grown human tissue. The external prosthesis of arm or leg that introduced restorative or normalizing technologies for the person has been reconceptualized to become a nerve stimulus that engenders the body's cooperation in manipulating as its own the simulated, lifelike, prosthetic device.

> The person may be understood as progressively being transformed into a technological replica, constituted not only by bionics, the application of biological principles to electronic design, but by artificial intelligence with simulated human intentionality.

The person may be understood as progressively being transformed into a technological replica, constituted not only by bionics, the application of biological principles to electronic design, but by artificial intelligence with simulated human intentionality. Williams (1997) notes that it is clear that the cyborg, post human, or transhuman is no longer just a creature of science fiction created by writers and filmmakers but is now represented in state of the art flight simulators and human pacemakers. He argues for the conceptualization of a cyborg or transhuman along a continuum—at one end or pole is the human organism and at the other is the pure machine (automaton) or artificial intelligence device. With the transformation of the human being by the addition of technologies, the location along the continuum changes toward the pure machine pole. In considering Williams' (1997) conceptualization, it is valid to ask, "At what point would the human being be regarded as machine?"

As radical as the proposition may seem, the temporal proximity of such a conceptualization has broad implications for nursing. To the extent that vital organs, perceived to constitute humanness, are progressively duplicated and present in an individual, it is valid to ask, "When is a person not a person?" Does the technological implant, integration, or replacement organ in a person actually become that person? Who would determine the degree of transformation? Is the technology regarded by the person as an aspect of self or as a technological part? How then, is wholeness of person, the concept of completeness of the self as a sentient human being, expressed? The elusive idea of mind resides for all intents and purposes in the brain. At this stage of human civilization, it is commonly accepted that in a living human being the successful severance, removal, and replacement of the human brain is not possible.

> **Does the technological implant, integration, or replacement organ in a person actually become that person?**

Guarding the City Walls

It is evident that when non-nursing derived techniques, theories, and methodologies are used in nursing research, the lexical terms with their extended discipline-specific meanings are superimposed on the thoughts and activities of the nurse and in outcomes of the research. In the reporting of research and in habitual use of the theories, non-nursing ideas and perspectives prevail over the philosophy of the nurse. This can be seen in the language used in research studies where researchers must necessarily report results using the terminology (and implied meanings) of the instrument or the methodology in order to achieve coherence (Purnell, 2003). Rosemary Ellis in Algase and Whall (1993) clearly articulated this problem:

> Nurse scholars employing, in toto, the substantive structure of another discipline to the study of phenomena encountered in nursing practice cannot necessarily claim that the products of their studies fit within the discipline of nursing. In other words, a nurse sociologist, for example, may at times generate sociological knowledge about a phenomenon, such as family, common to nursing and sociology. In this situation, the distinction (or overlap, if possible) between what is nursing knowledge and what is sociological knowledge rests in the relevance of the knowledge to the *purposes* or beneficence of nursing practice *and* in the congruence between *values and methods* between nursing and sociology. (p. 70)

Technology in nursing is defined and understood in terms of components prescribed outside of the discipline of nursing and in terms contrary to the notion of wholeness of person. A similar dilemma may be seen in the exemplars associated with the reductionist philosophy interpolated into the discipline of nursing under the guise of "borrowed" behaviorist theories, such as Azjen and Fishbein's theory of reasoned action (1980). Behaviorism may be understood as a cluster of doctrines based on the belief that behavior is fundamental to understanding mental phenomena. Various tenets of behaviorism may still be seen today in nursing theories and research instruments that have their underlying philosophy in the notion of behaviorism, and as such are contrary in their essence to the philosophy of nursing and nursing intentionality.

> 66 Intentionality is a fundamental human dynamic that provides the context through which human-beings value, order, and live out the meaning of their lives in caring relationships among themselves, their environment, and the universe (Purnell, 2003) 99

Intentionality in Nursing

Intentionality is a fundamental human dynamic that provides the context through which human-beings value, order, and live out the meaning of their lives in caring relationships among themselves, their environment, and the universe (Purnell, 2003). Intentionality is also a subtle organizing influence, energy, and dimension. In nursing, intentionality becomes an active matrix extending from the unconscious to the conscious for the actualization of nursing. In praxis, the caring potential of nursing intentionality is fulfilled and transformed. The intention of nursing is for beneficence and the greater good and is expressed in its philosophy (Purnell, 2003). Ellis succinctly stated in Algase and Whall (1993) that "As nurses first, scholars of the discipline understand the good or beneficence that the practice of nursing aims to contribute to society" (p. 69).

The growth and transformation of the ontology and epistemology are closely connected with disciplinary identity and are centered on the intentionality of the discipline (Purnell, 2003). The intention of the discipline is recognized with the introduction and development of new ideas that eventually challenge the metaparadigm. As perceived knowledge becomes better accepted, critically tested, and examined, it becomes highly complex, with the energy and approval of the discipline vested in the intent to adopt the knowledge. Evaluation and approval through aesthetic discernment of the discipline are the means by which the knowledge becomes received knowledge and is integrated back into human and disciplinary knowledge bases. The metaparadigm may thus be understood as the general expression of nursing intentionality. However, as a discipline and profession, the development of nursing has included the adaptation and use of epistemic knowledge from other disciplines that is incongruent with the philosophic foundation of nursing (Kikuchi & Simmons, 1992; Polifroni & Packard, 1993).

Technology as Domain Concept?

Is the person or recipient of biomedical technology, therefore, reducible by the technological part? Does this part present a conflict with the philosophy of nursing that reflects wholeness as integral to the nature of person? It seems that with this argument, a reductionist worldview has already been imprinted, forced by the philosophy of technology already embodied in the biomedical part, and added into the human being.

The situation is a double-edged sword. On the one hand, the nature and substance of biotechnology argues for non-inclusion of technology as a domain concept in nursing simply because it is not nursing technology, that is, it does not come forth from nursing nor does it embody the philosophy of nursing. On the other hand, when biotechnologies are integrated into the person, the situation argues for inclusion of technology as a domain concept either as person or as technology and person. However, can the technology be considered as an aspect of a person from a nursing viewpoint or as a part or unit of the person from a reductionist viewpoint?

Technology or Humanology?

Gadow (1984) observes that objects such as computers and bureaucracies seem to have a life of their own. She declares, "In that way, they are radically other, they resist being assimilated into the individuality of a human life" (p. 64). However, not only do they resist becoming integral to a human life, they become independent, invisible forces to be reckoned with. For example, a major computer manufacturer is marketing the idea of "humanology," a so-called science that caters to the needs of human beings from the point of view of technology (Hewlett Packard, 2003). Technology, with the self-attributed charisma of persons, appears now to command the services of human advocates. It also appears that the philosophy of reductionism, inherent in biomedical technology, has gained an uncommon power by this inversion of role and of perspective.

> " To begin to address the numerous questions that arise from the consideration of the integration of technology and human beings, it is necessary to transcend the present and future trajectories and attend to the foundational values that are intentionally expressed in nursing, in every thought, intuition, deliberation, action, and reflection. "

In considering the role of medical technology, Williams (1997) suggests viewing technology through the lens of three interrelated levels. The first level to consider is the extent to which medical technologies transform or render human bodies increasingly uncertain. The second level is the type of analysis generated by the notion of the embodiment of a cyborg in a technologically mediated age. The final and broader level considers the issues caused by the conflict between the modernist enterprise of medicine and the present, post-modern, contemporary medical practice. According to Williams, current developments in medical technology represent a continuation of modernist imperatives that center on rational control and the domination of nature—that is, the human being.

The implications for nursing are profound and extend from practice issues at the bedside to philosophical consideration of the human being as reformed, restructured, or reconstituted by technology. To what extent is the person "technologized" and subtly controlled? When is a person not a person? How will the notion of embodied technology be integrated into the domain of nursing—in the paradigmatic concept of the person being nursed? Is the technology thus regarded as person? What is the perspective of the person being nursed? Does the person regard the technology as self?

How does the technology influence the wholeness of person? Does the technology render the person "whole," more than whole, or less than whole? What does the concept of wholeness mean when technology is involved in the consideration? To begin to address the numerous questions that arise from the consideration of the integration of technology and human beings, it is necessary to transcend the present and future trajectories and attend to the foundational values that are intentionally expressed in nursing, in every thought, intuition, deliberation, action, and reflection.

> "The implications for nursing are profound and extend from practice issues at the bedside to philosophical consideration of the human being as reformed, restructured, or reconstituted by technology."

Intentionality and Reductionism

The implications drive deeper and are concerned with the underlying intentionality of the medical technologists and engineers who design, create, and construct technology for insertion or integration into the human being or for the environment. Underpinned by a reductionist philosophy, the domain boundaries of the technology in medicine are not at the interface of person and technology but in the scope of the implications with regard to risk, to commoditization, and to moral and legal issues. For example, who will own the implanted part if it is not paid for by the person into whom it is inserted? Who will or can inherit the part at the person's death? Can the part be separated involuntarily from the person?

It can be seen from this discussion that boundaries between person and technology are already at the stage of being indefinable. From this point of view, technology may well be subsumed into the metaparadigm under the concept of person or be regarded as a sub concept.

However, from the point of view that the technology is a *part* and not *the* human-being, could it then be included under the external environment of person, along with other environmental technology? Alternately, are the person and environment more closely linked through the environment of embedded technology? The extreme nature of this argument underscores the need for a line to be drawn, but where?

Nursing and Holism

Holism in nursing is the unique perspective of nursing (Hayes, 1992). In nursing, concern for the wholeness of person is expressed in philosophies of nursing that are integrated into theories, research, and practice. Holism is the notion that an integrated whole has a reality independent of, and greater than, the sum of its parts (Dossey, 1988). The holistic perspective is one in which human beings are understood as unified wholes, are greater than the sum of their parts, and are therefore irreducible. What affects and influences one aspect of the person influences the whole person in unique ways. Nursing's Social Policy Statement, which articulates a framework for understanding nursing's relationship with society, states that "Humans manifest an essential unity of mind/body/spirit" (American Nurses Association, 1995, p. 3).

> Holism is the notion that an integrated whole has a reality independent of, and greater than, the sum of its parts.

As a concept, holism was first coined by Jan Christian Smuts in 1926. Smuts, a South African public official with avid interests in biology and philosophy, disagreed with the analytic method of studying organisms. He felt that the reductive method of studying in isolation each body part, such as a cell or organ, did not address the fundamental harmony of the whole organism and the integrated way that the organism maintained itself in a fluctuating environment (Blattner, 1981). Smuts termed the continuing process of organizing as "holism."

In nursing, while diverse understandings contribute a variety of meanings to holism, all convey the idea of the whole person, dimensions of which include interrelated concepts such as mind-body-spirit and internal and external environments. Holism includes the idea of a harmonious balance within and among human-beings interacting in participatory relationships with themselves, the environment, and the universe. While mainstream conceptions differ about the nature of holistic perspectives, these conceptions are united in holding opposition to the philosophy of reductionism that regards the human being as a mere collection or repository of parts. In order to explore conceptually situating technology within the metaparadigm of nursing, an overview of several domain concepts follows:

Situating Technology Within the Metaparadigm

The Domain of Nursing

All disciplines are formed around a domain of unique knowledge that has theoretical and practical boundaries. This domain of knowledge is "the crux of the discipline" (Meleis, 1997, p. 102). Theoretical boundaries are created by current concerns and visionary questions upon which the members of the discipline focus. Practical boundaries represent the current state of research evolving out of these questions. Various aspects of the domain are more changeable, such as the way phenomena are conceptualized and the nature of questions asked about them. While the interests of some disciplines may overlap the interests of another, the primacy or centrality of the interest to the discipline determines the domain affiliation.

Paradigms

Paradigms are epistemological systems that can "describe a set of relations in such a way that symbolic representation appears to map a complex phenomena, but it is merely the product of the reflective activity of the paradigm describer, who may try to say how it was but could never promise how it will be (Grumet, 1990). Thomas Kuhn (1962), who popularized the concept of the paradigm, revealed in a later postscript to his work that the term "paradigm" had been used in several different senses: On the one hand, it stood for an entire constellation of beliefs, values, and techniques shared by the members of a scientific community; on the other hand, the term also represented one kind of element in that constellation. However, he also invested the term paradigm with a third, more concrete meaning: an exemplar, or classic example, intended to assist developing scientists (Kuhn, 1977b). It is this description that Kuhn felt more correctly conveyed the correct meaning of the word and of the concept.

Metaparadigms

Created by Masterman in 1970, the *metaparadigm* is "simply a synonym coined for the metaphysical connotation of a disciplinary matrix and its exemplars" (Rawnsley, 1996, p. 106). Metaparadigms, or constellations of beliefs, are described as being made up of concepts that identify the phenomena of interest to a discipline and of global propositions that constitute a framework of relationships among the phenomena. These conceptual structures include major philosophical worldviews of the discipline and set forth domain boundaries. Rawnsley (1996) notes that the idea of the metaparadigm was introduced into the nursing literature at a time when the discipline was defending its new status as a science.

Perspectives on Core Domain Concepts

Contemporary nursing literature documents domain concepts of the nurse-patient dyad, the nurse-patient relationship, and the phenomenon of caring. However, within a generally accepted conception of the metaparadigm of nursing knowledge that includes person (client), environment, health, and nursing (Fawcett, 1998; Monti & Tingen, 1999), the *nurse, technology*, and *caring* are conspicuously absent. This particular paradigm, although disputed by many scholars (Kim, 1987; Leininger, 1991; Newman, Sime, & Corcoran-Perry, 1992; Watson, 1990), has been taught to students by nursing educators for decades.

Several perspectives of core domain concepts therefore compete for primacy within the discipline of nursing (Conway, 1985). Among Fawcett's concepts, person refers to the recipient of nursing and extends from individuals to families, communities, and other groups. Importantly, Fawcett's concepts do not refer to the nurse as the enactor or creator of nursing. Environment includes significant others and the physical surroundings in which nursing takes place, along with society as a whole. Health, the state of a person's well-being, can range from high-level wellness to terminal illness. Nursing refers to actions taken by nurses on behalf of the person and to the goals or outcomes of those actions. Fawcett later introduced these concepts, along with four relational propositions, as the metaparadigm of nursing.

In an invitation to dialogue, Fawcett (1996) identified four requirements for the metaparadigm of any discipline. These are first, that a metaparadigm must identify a unique domain for inquiry and practice; second, a metaparadigm must encompass all the phenomena of the discipline parsimoniously; third, a metaparadigm must be "perspective neutral" (p. 94); and fourth, a metaparadigm must be international in scope and substance—it cannot reflect a particular national, cultural, or ethnic belief and value. Fawcett claimed that these four criteria may be used to evaluate any proposal for metaparadigm concepts and propositions.

Propositions operationalizing these concepts for nursing describe the following links: the link to person and health, stating that the discipline of nursing is concerned with principles and laws governing the life process, well-being, and optimal well-being of human beings, sick or well; the interaction between person and environment, which states that the discipline of nursing is concerned with humans interacting with the environment in normal life events and in critical life situations; the link between health and nursing, which declares that the discipline of nursing is concerned with the nursing actions by which positive changes in health status are affected; the link between wholeness and health of human beings, which describes the interaction between nurse and environment; and the link between person, environment, and health, which acknowledges that they are interactive with the environment.

It is evident that these phenomena are in no way standardized, nor do they engender general agreement within the discipline. Cody (1996) observes that exclusions from Fawcett's view include theories focused on caring, the concept of persons being studied who are not recipients of nursing, the concept of health when it is not regarded as a state or a continuum of low- to high-level wellness, and the concept of nursing when it is not regarded as the traditional nursing process (p. 98). The nurse as person is not conceptualized and remains as a shadowy dispenser of nursing actions.

Meleis (1997) offers a different set of domain concepts. According to Meleis, central components of the domain of nursing are (a) major concepts and problems of the field; (b) processes for assessment, diagnosis, and intervention; (c) tools to assess, diagnose, and intervene; and (d) research designs and methodologies that are most congruent with nursing knowledge. Significantly, Meleis notes that the theoretical boundaries of the domain of nursing are the result of explication of the first three central components.

> Nursing cannot be defined by its concepts while simultaneously being included as one of the concepts.

Meleis asserts that seven central, dynamic concepts constitute the domain of nursing knowledge: "The nurse interacts *(interaction)* with a human being in a health/illness situation *(nursing client)* who is in an integral part of his sociocultural context *(environment)* and who is in some sort of transition or is anticipating a transition *(transition)*; the nurse-patient interactions are organized around some purpose *(nursing process, problem solving, holistic assessment,* or *caring actions)*, and the nurse uses some actions *(nursing therapeutics)* to enhance, bring about, or facilitate health *(health)* (p. 106). Meleis argues that theories developed based on any of these concepts are nursing theories when the ultimate goal is concerned with the maintenance, promotion, or facilitation of health and well-being

Both Meleis (1997) and Conway (1985) take exception to the concept of nursing as a domain concept, since it represents a tautology: Nursing cannot be defined by its concepts while simultaneously being included as one of the concepts (Reed, 1996). Caring is included in several domain conceptualizations (Boykin & Schoenhofer, 2001; Leininger, 1991; Morse et al.,1990). While caring has been contested as a domain concept on the grounds that it pertains to a particular viewpoint (Meleis, 1997), Malinski argues for its conceptual validity in her assertion that the existence of caring behaviors generalizes across all cultures.

Valuing and Prizing the Common Good

The examples above display the intricate valuing of the discipline evinced by scholars of nursing. Regardless of the conceptual difficulties arising from different perspectives, the common philosophical stance is to do or create good in the best way possible through nursing, however nursing and the good is conceptualized. The paradigmatic concepts that represent the domain of nursing, however diverse, may therefore be said to be unified by the intentionality of the discipline and express the vision of nursing for the common good. Ellis (Algase & Whall, 1993) succinctly stated, "As nurses first, scholars of the discipline understand the good or beneficence that the practice of nursing aims to contribute to society" (p. 69).

> Regardless of the conceptual difficulties arising from different perspectives, the common philosophical stance is to do or create good in the best way possible through nursing, however nursing and the good is conceptualized.

Coercion by Non-Nursing Philosophical Constructs

While the metaparadigm of nursing sets forth the philosophical constructs of nursing for theory, research, and practice, the use of non-nursing theories and research methodologies is, in effect, a practice of turning away from their guidance for the sake of outcomes. The advent of the electronic age in the 1980s and 1990s clouded the identification of disciplinary origins of contemporary perspectives. Information is rapidly shared across geographical and virtual borders and across conceptual boundaries among disciplines of knowledge. Nurse researchers regularly collaborate with researchers from other disciplines in studies of mutual interest and jointly publish their findings in the media of multiple associated discplines. Nurse-authors are customarily not identified by their professional credentials outside of the nursing literature, and, as professional nurses, become unidentifiable as progenitors of knowledge.

Therefore, although various theories may seem ideal for certain research studies in nursing, the language, study, and outcomes are frequently biased toward the underlying reductionist philosophy. The allure in nursing of ready-made, testable theories and instruments facilitates their adoption and increased frequency of use. The practice over time of turning to a frequently used non-nursing research methodology or instrument can offer a false sense of security. Unless instruments are redesigned or refocused to embrace a nursing stance, incorporating a philosophy of wholeness of person, the biased results of the research are cycled into the epistemology and ontology of nursing. If the epistemic foundations are unexamined, that which is uniquely nursing, that is, the ontology of nursing, is diluted or lost.

> Technology in nursing, both intracorporreal and extracorporreal, is integral to the nursing situation, from where all nursing knowledge arises. "

The implications for adoption of biomedical technology and its embodied reductionist philosophy extend beyond those of theories and research instruments that originate in other disciplines. The influence of technology in nursing lies in its ability to subtly bend and coerce pre-theoretical thought. Technology in nursing, both intracorporreal and extracorporreal, is integral to the nursing situation, from where all nursing knowledge arises (Boykin & Schoenhofer, 2001). This nursing knowledge is conceptualized in domain concepts to guide nursing theory, research, practice, and education. The understanding that technology is not an acknowledged domain concept does not hinder the development of theory and research related to it and to the nurse and caring. Caught in the breach, these concepts directly concern contemporary nursing practice. This has resulted in theories and research continuing without the guidance of domain concepts and without the sanction of public funding. Consequently, barriers are presented with the paucity of research funding and with the difficult application of research methods to what is a complex and philosophically enigmatic concept. The lack of attention can be construed as further tacit devaluation of the role of nurses and of the "value-added" (Boykin & Schoenhofer, 1997) nature of nursing in nurturing the wholeness of person in the mediating, integrating, and rendering invisible of medical technology in practice.

Technology in Nursing, or Nursing Technology?

Thus far, only biomedical technology originating from medicine and used in nursing has been examined. What then is nursing technology? Are any technologies designed and created by nursing that may be understood as unique to nursing and in nursing?

Ellis (Pressler & Fitzpatrick, 1988) felt that the field of inquiry in nursing included four types of nursing knowledge: scientific nursing knowledge, historical nursing knowledge, philosophical nursing knowledge; and nursing technology. Ellis described nursing technology as a major type for knowledge inquiry. She described nursing technology as "those techniques performed in the context and actuality of nursing practice" (Pressler & Fitzpatrick, 1988, p. 29). Nursing techniques were described as therapeutic, interpersonal techniques; development of nursing care procedures; and educational techniques used with clients. She also considered research concerning nursing technology as "being essential to understand the artistry of practice" (Pressler & Fitzpatrick, 1988, p. 29). Examples of nursing technology per se, were not found, although examples of biotechnology used in nursing proliferate.

Biotechnology as a Nursing Technology?

In order to evaluate the possibility of biotechnology being recognized as a nursing technology, the philosophical pedigree of the technology must be carefully examined. Has a nurse designed and created the technology for nurturing the one cared for from a perspective of holism? Is the technology whole-patient focused? Is the nature of the technology such that personhood is enhanced within the context of the nursing situation? Is the intention realized of both the nurse and the patient? Boykin and Schoenhofer (1997) state:

> Nursing practice grounded in the importance of person-as-person, of person-as-caring, and of person-as-whole-in-the-moment would result in outcomes of care—or experiences of being cared for—that are in context of person. What is experienced as the result of care would reflect characteristics of personhood: unity—creative evolving of a unifying, consistent, whole awareness—creative unfolding of a recognizable self; and intention, blending desire and purpose (p. 61).

Thus the authenticity and the essentiality of nursing are uniquely located in the caring relationship that is participated in by the nurse and the one nursed. By definition, medical technologies do not contribute to caring for the person. The intentionality of the nurse is to do good (Algase & Whall, 1993; Purnell, 2003) and to nurture the wholeness of person (Boykin & Schoenhofer, 2001).

> *... Overwhelming demands are placed upon the nurse to be technologically competent, and the authentic intention of the nurse to know persons in their wholeness is often devalued.*

Locsin's (2001) focus on technological competency as caring illuminates the tension between the nurse, the technology, and the patient. According to Locsin, overwhelming demands are placed upon the nurse to be technologically competent, and the authentic intention of the nurse to know persons in their wholeness is often devalued. While responding to the patient, the nurse is challenged to be technologically proficient. Locsin declares, "Such authenticity and intentionality are demonstrated when the nurse, with all the demands of technological expertise, accepts the patient fully as a human being, not as an object" (p. 93).

Locsin (2001) underscores the importance of the role of intentionality in nursing, and of its importance in tacitly distinguishing the domain of nursing. He states:

> Technological competency demonstrated from a perspective not grounded in nursing is the ultimate impersonation of a nurse: *simply being technologically competent is not nursing.* Nursing occurs in situations when technologies are exercised proficiently with the authentic intention to know patients fully as persons who are in the process of living and growing in caring (Boykin & Schoenhofer, 1993). When viewed from this nursing perspective, technological competency as an expression of caring is truly nursing (p. 94).

This example also emphasizes the role of intentionality with embedded values as a guiding framework for practice and illuminates Benner and Wrubel's (1989) understanding of precognitive forms of intentionality exhibited by the expert nurse. These are meaningful, purposeful behaviors. In particular, technological competency enables smooth functioning without elaborate conscious deliberation, thus rendering the technology "invisible."

Summary

The issues explored concerning technology, caring, and intentionality in nursing have been seen as intertwined and not able to be regarded as discrete concepts for analysis. The reality that all concepts are co-experienced and interrelated in nursing should provide an indication of their complexity and need for acknowledgement in the domain as interrelated core concepts. The provocative issues of today will be the commonplace tomorrow, especially where technology is concerned.

In consideration of technology as an interrelated domain concept then, we are also bound to consider the nurse and caring as uniquely bound up in the solution. We are also bound to acknowledge that scholarly debate must rise above technology as object, technique, virtual and information technology, or human emulation. Epistemological considerations for practice, theory, and research that began this discussion have led us to the ontological core of nursing that is bound up in intentional valuing and prizing of person, articulated in nursing philosophies and expressed in a humane stance of caring. The solutions might be found in consideration of our final question: Can the intentionality that nurtures the wholeness of person transcend the reductionistic nature of technology and unify the disciplines within the therapeutic caring relationship that is nursing? If so, the contents of our metaphorical Trojan Horse will have been rendered harmless.

Learning From the Past— A Myth Revisited

Imagine if the myth had gone like this:

> Evening fell, and the huge horse stood, poised and waiting in the heart of the city where the townspeople had proudly escorted it. "Look at our new possession," they exclaimed, "The world will envy us." And they stood and speculated and thought of all the different uses to which they could put the wooden horse. "We can use it to see over the city walls and communicate with our neighbors," said one. Another said, "We might be able to conquer our enemies with it." And yet another exclaimed, "Let us polish and preserve it so that it will last forever and keep our children safe!" But not all the townspeople were fooled. By the light of the moon, they crept up to the gift horse and waited. The belly of the horse opened, and foreign soldiers spilled out. With a cry, the townspeople pounced and overcame the invaders. The threat to the city was no more.

References

Azjen, I. (1985). From intention to actions: A theory of planned behavior. In J. Kuhl & J. Beckmann (Eds.), *Action control: From cognition to behavior* (pp. 11-39). Berlin, Germany: Springer Verlag.

Ajzen, I. (1991). The theory of planned behavior. *Organizational Behavior and Human Decision Processes, 50,* 179-211.

Ajzen, I., & Fishbein, M. (1980). *Understanding attitudes and predicting social behavior.* Englewood Cliffs, NJ: Prentice-Hall.

Algase, D.L., & Whall, A.F. (1993). Rosemary Ellis' views on the substantive structure of nursing. *Image: Journal of Nursing Scholarship, 25*(1), 69-72.

American Nurses Association. (1995). *Nursing's social policy statement.* Washington, DC: Author.

Barnard, A. (1999). Nursing and the primacy of technological progress. *International Journal of Nursing Studies, 36,* 435-442.

Benner, P., & Wrubel, J. (1989). *The primacy of caring: Stress and coping in health and illness.* Menlo Park, CA: Addison-Wesley.

Blattner, B. (1981). *Holistic nursing.* Englewood Cliffs, NJ: Prentice-Hall,

Boykin, A., & Schoenhofer, S.O. (1997). Reframing outcomes: Enhancing personhood. *Advanced Nursing Practice, 3*(1), 60-65.

Boykin, A., & Schoenhofer, S.O. (2001). *Nursing as caring: A model for transforming practice* (2nd ed.). New York: Jones & Bartlett, National League for Nursing Press.

Cody, W.K. (1996). On the requirements for a metaparadigm: An invitation to dialogue. Response. *Nursing Science Quarterly, 9*(3), 97-99.

Conway, M.E. (1985). Toward greater specificity in defining nursing's metaparadigm. *Advances in Nursing Science, 7*(4), 73-81.

Cooper, M.C. (1993). The intersection of technology and care in the ICU. *Advances in Nursing Science, 15,* 23-32.

Dossey, B.M., Keegan, L., Guzzetta, C.E., & Kolkmeier, L.G. (1988). *Holistic nursing: A handbook for practice.* Rockville, MD: Aspen.

Ellis, R. (1983). Philosophic inquiry. In H.H. Werley & J.J. Fitzpatrick (Eds.), *Annual review of nursing research* (Vol. 1; pp. 211-228). New York: Springer.

Fawcett, J. (1996). On the requirements for a metaparadigm: An invitation to dialogue. Commentary. *Nursing Science Quarterly, 9*(3), 94-97.

Gadow, S. (1984). Touch and technology: Two paradigms of patient care. *Journal of Religion and Health, 23*(1), 63-69.

Hewlett Packard. (2003). HP Website. Retrieved September 12, 2003, from http://www.hp.com.

Kikuchi, J.R., & Simmons, H. (1992). *Philosophic inquiry in nursing.* Thousand Oaks, CA: Sage.

Kim, H.S. (1987). Structuring the nursing knowledge system: A typology of four domains. *Scholarly Inquiry for Nursing Practice, 1,* 99-110.

Kuhn, T.S. (1962). *The structure of scientific revolutions* (3rd ed.). Chicago: University of Chicago Press.

Kuhn, T.S. (1977a). Second thoughts on paradigms. In F. Suppe (Ed.), *The structure of scientific theories* (2nd ed.), pp. 459-517. Urbana, IL: University of Illinois Press.

Kuhn, T.S. (1977b). *The essential tension.* Chicago, IL: University of Chicago Press.

Leininger, M.M. (1991). The theory of culture care diversity and universality. In M.M. Leininger (Ed.), *Culture care diversity and universality: A theory of nursing*. New York: National League for Nursing.

Locsin, R.C. (1995). Machine technologies and caring in nursing. *Image: Journal of Nursing Scholarship, 27*(3), 201-203.

Locsin, R.C. (2001). *Advancing technology, caring, and nursing*. Westport, CT: Auburn House.

Malinski, V.M. (1996). On the requirements for a metaparadigm: An invitation to dialogue. Response. *Nursing Science Quarterly, 9*(3), 100-102.

McConnell, E.A. (1998). The coalescence of technology and humanism in nursing practice: It just doesn't happen and it doesn't come easily. *Holistic Nursing Practice, 12*, 23-30.

Meleis, A.I. (1997). *Theoretical nursing: Development and progress* (3rd ed.). Philadelphia: Lippincott-Raven.

Monti, E.J., & Tingen, M.S. (1999). Multiple paradigms of nursing science. *Advances in Nursing Science, 21*(4), 64-80.

Morse, J.M., Solberg, S.M., Neander, W.L., Bottorff, J.L., & Johnson, J.L. (1990). Concepts of caring and caring as a concept. *Advances in Nursing Science, 13*(1), 1-14.

Newman, M.A., Sime, A.M., & Corcoran-Perry, S.A. (1991). The focus of the discipline of nursing. *Advances in Nursing Science, 14*(1), 1-6.

Phenix, P.H. (1964). *Realms of meaning*. New York: McGraw Hill.

Polifroni, E.C., & Packard, S. (1993). Psychological determinism and the evolving nursing paradigm. *Nursing Science Quarterly, 6*(2), 63-68.

Pressler, J.L., & Fitzpatrick, J.J. (1988). Contributions of Rosemary Ellis to knowledge development for nursing. *Image: Journal of Nursing Scholarship, 20*(1), 28-30.

Purnell, M.J. (1998). Who really makes the bed? Uncovering technological dissonance in nursing. *Holistic Nursing Practice, 12,* 12-22.

Purnell, M.J. (2003). *Intentionality in nursing: A foundational inquiry.* Doctoral dissertation, University of Miami, Florida.

Purnell, M.J., Horner, D., Gonzalez, J., & Westman, N. (2001). The nursing shortage: Revisioning the future. *Journal of Nursing Administration, 31*(4), 79-86.

Rawnsley, M.M. (1996). On the requirements for a metaparadigm: An invitation to dialogue. Response. *Nursing Science Quarterly, 9*(3), 102-106.

Ray, M.A. (1987). Technological caring: A new model in critical care. *Dimensions of Critical Care Nursing, 6,* 166-173.

Reed, P. (1997). Nursing: The ontology of the discipline. *Nursing Science Quarterly, 10*(2), 76-79.

Sigma Theta Tau International. (2003). The Society's vision and mission. Retrieved September 12, 2003, from http://www.nursingsociety.org/about/overview.html

Thorne, S., Canam, C., Dahinten, S., Hall, W., Henderson, A., & Kirkham, S. (1998). Nursing's metaparadigm concepts. *Journal of Advanced Nursing, 27*(6), 1257-1268.

Walters, A.J. (1995). Technology and the lifeworld of critical care nursing. *Journal of Advanced Nursing, 22,* 338-346.

Watson, J. (1991). Caring knowledge and informed moral passion. *Advances in Nursing Science, 13*(1), 15-24.

Weber, D.O. (2002). The next little thing. *Health Forum Journal, 45*(5), 10-16.

Williams, S.J. (1997). Modern medicine and the "uncertain body:" From corporeality to hyppereality? *Social Science and Medicine, 45,* 1041-1049.

> The interactive nature of caring requires mutual
> commitment from the one giving care and the one
> being cared for.

4

CHAPTER

Caring in Nursing and its Symbiosis with Technology

By Rozzano C. Locsin

Caring as a substantive knowledge of nursing directs attention to its description and its many conceptualizations in the practice of nursing. The pressure for professional nurses to achieve greater technological proficiency has fostered a rethinking of the technology-caring dichotomy. Caring has gained prominence as a central expression of nursing. The current emphasis on technologic competency for quality nursing practice and the dependence upon machine technology has achieved a distinction that is significant to the practice of nursing. To fully care within this increasingly sophisticated world, nurses seem to recognize that technologic proficiency is a desirable attribute—not a substitute for caring but an enhancement of caring.

The issues that exist about caring in nursing include caring as the essence of nursing, caring as the tradition of nursing, and caring as a process of interaction and communication in nursing. Caring in nursing is described in a variety of ways (Leininger, 1988; Watson, 1985). Discussions of the issues of caring in nursing (Jacono, 1993; Olson, 1993; Phillips, 1993; Swanson, 1993), attributes of caring (Roach, 1987), and ingredients of caring (Mayeroff, 1971) all illustrate the significance of the concept of caring. Lynaugh and Fagin (1988) support Leininger's (1988) claim that caring is the unifying feature of nursing. Leininger also states that caring is the common link that brings nurses together. In like manner, Watson (1990) emphasizes that caring is the moral ideal of nursing, while Roach (1992) considers caring to be a human mode of being.

Some of the dimensions of caring in nursing include caring as the tradition of nursing (Olson, 1993) and caring as a process of interaction (Phillips, 1993). Mangold (1991) defined caring as assisting others' growth in a cognitive and emotional sense toward self-actualization. Noddings (1984), however, suggested that caring occurs when one is completely receptive to another: The interactive nature of caring requires mutual commitment from the one giving care and the one being cared for. Phillips (1993) described caring in nursing as requiring the one giving care to respond to the needs of another. Boykin and Schoenhofer (2001) describe caring as being intentionally and authentically present for another.

The regard for caring in nursing as the field's special knowledge has been claimed by Olson (1993) as the path that professionalization of nursing follow in order to establish itself as a fully-fledged profession. Porter (1992) emphasized, "One of the most consistent strategies to achieve professionalization of nursing has been the attempt to acquire a unique knowledge base" (p. 72). The possession of such knowledge is being seen as one of the essential traits of a "true" profession.

To address the issue that caring has traditionally constituted nursing practice activities, Olson (1993) studied achievement evaluations of nurses at St. Luke's hospital from 1915-1937. It was found that performance of nurses were frequently evaluated and valued in terms of how they "controlled," "managed," and handled patients aiming at a discernible outcome of "neat, finished-appearing work" (p. 71). These activities were more valuable to nursing supervisors than those that reflect person-oriented actions. If caring traditionally constituted nursing practice, the evidence contradicts the claim. Like the first three decades of the 1900s, nursing practice continues to be prized or evaluated using task-orientations, performance of procedures, and trustworthiness in following practice instructions. Echoing these findings, Cody (1995) declares that people have made many non-nursing tasks matter in nursing. These tasks, such as making beds and transcribing patient-care medication prescriptions, were included in job descriptions to the extent that these tasks are the job expectations. Of greater importance is the appreciation of tasks in which many nurses consider these tasks to be "nursing."

As an interaction and communication issue, Noddings (1984) explained that caring occurs when one is receptive of the other completely. This depiction is also shared by Phillips (1993), who described caring as "an interactive process which requires the carer to be responsive to the needs of the person cared for, the resources available, and the context in which care occurs" (p. 1558). This aroused the proclamation that "the word 'caring' does have emotional connotations and that its present emphasis, possibly a reaction to the increasing use of technology in nursing, may re-create the impression, assuming it was never dispelled, that what is often called 'basic' or 'low tech,' nursing does not require high levels of cognitive processing" (p. 1557). The connotation of the interactive nature of caring as simply "co-responsiveness" in the light of relationships is a minimalist presentation of that which transpires between the nurse and the patient.

The meaning of caring in nursing practice is expanded to include two dichotomous but integral concepts, that which pertains to the duty to care for others and the right to control one's own activities in the name of caring. Succinctly expressed, nurses are expected to act out of an obligation or duty to consider caring more as an identity than as a job and to express humanitarianism without thought of autonomy either at the bedside or in their profession (Reverby, 1987).

The issue of duty to care and the right to own one's activities has affected many contemporary issues of strategizing political empowerment and influencing organizational change. Paley (2001), questioning the legitimacy of caring, declared that "knowledge of caring is an aggregate of things said about it, derived from a potentially endless series of associations, grouped into attributes on the basis of resemblances, and conceived as a holistic description of the phenomenon." Reacting to Paley's (2001) claims about caring in nursing is not advanced by research, and that nursing merely generates endless lists of terms to describe caring (p. 96).

> Succinctly expressed, nurses are expected to act out of an obligation or duty to consider caring more as an identity than as a job and to express humanitarianism without thought of autonomy either at the bedside or in their profession

Edwards (2001) explained the distinction between intentional and ontological care. Intentional caring is a set of voluntary, deliberate actions on the part of human beings, while ontological care is a form of care which all humans, by definition, must instantiate, featuring the constitution of all human species.

Nursing's educational philosophy, ideological underpinnings, and structured positions have made it difficult to create circumstances within which to gain recognition of caring values. Emphasis on educational attainment as the preferred route to professionalization has achieved contradictory responses from nurses. The nursing community continues to struggle with the basis for and the value of caring, while many nurses continue to hope that with more education, explicit theories to explain the scientific basis for nursing, new skills, and a lot of assertiveness training, the nursing community will change in its view of professional nursing, bureaucratic nursing, and technical nursing. The focus of nursing practice has become the beckoning cry as it influences the theoretical foundations of nursing. It is the creation of the conditions under which caring is valued that these perspectives are realized. Situations where nursing occurs have been described as the "caring moment" (Watson, 1985), the "now moment" (Parse, 1987), the "between" (Paterson and Zderad, 1988), the "caring between" (Boykin and Schoenhofer, 2001), and the "co-created moment" (Locsin, 1997). Within the present conditions, many nurses find themselves forced to abandon the effort to care or to abandon nursing altogether. The issue of autonomy of practice becomes an exercise in futility when the practice of nursing is reduced to simply following procedures and to proficiency with technologies.

How do patients perceive caring? Burfitt et al (1993) reviewed various published materials and drew the following:

- Caring is when as a person (residents/patients) I am being listened to; [when it is] being recognized that I have my own way of thinking and establishing caring relationships; [when] it is realized that I know I need and must receive care when I cannot do it myself anymore; [when] it is recognized that I have ideas of how to live a life in a long-term care facility (Aventuro, 1991).

- Caring is when others recognize my individual qualities and needs, [provide a] reassuring presence, provide information, demonstrate professional knowledge and skills, assist with pain alleviation, and promote autonomy (Brown, 1986).

- Caring is nursing actions that focus on physical care including teaching (Cronin and Harrison, 1988).

- Caring involves vigilance (constancy, tasks, time, and talk) and mutuality (sensing, trust, respect, and shared humanity) (Greiner and Harris, 1992)

- Caring is protecting, supporting, confirming, and transcending (Hutchinson and Bahr, 1991).

- Caring is knowing when to call the doctor and follow-through. It is demonstrated competency of skills and accessibility and the recognition of the patient's need for a trusting relationship (Keane, Chastain, & Rudisill, 1987).

- Caring means health teaching, assessment, physical care, advocacy, knowledge, supplying resources, planning for future, and safety. As a relationship, it is concern, progress, hope, listening, personal relationship, building self-esteem, touching, laughter, and humor (Knowlden, 1985).

- Caring is competency in clinical knowledge (Larson, 1984; Mayer, 1986).

- Caring is descriptive of a mutual process in which intentions are joined to form a shared experience. In this mutual process, healing is an outcome that might otherwise be elusive (Burfitt, et al., 1993).

> Nursing is accomplished through acting on the informed intention to care in creative ways that are personally and situationally meaningful.

Grounding the model of technological competency as caring in nursing is the theory of Nursing as Caring (Boykin and Schoenhofer, 2001). Although not inclusive, Burfitt's summary portrayed an array of caring views tantamount to describing the magnitude from which the concept of caring has been studied and has influenced nursing as a practice discipline and has been perceived by patients. However, not everyone in nursing agrees to the unity that is envisioned with caring in nursing. Phillips (1993) advanced the conclusion that nursing skills will not be explained by further analysis of the concept of care or promulgated by the connotations of the word. This argument, being founded by contentions that caring is aimed at explaining the complex process of nursing and of the pervasive use of the word caring as synonymous with nursing, only contributed to the erroneous emphasis in general nursing on emotional caring, thus perpetuating the fallacious thought-of distinction between caring and curing. Likened to teaching, Phillips distinctly exhibited this delineation of caring. It is a task defined by the intention of the actor. However, the evaluation of its success is more complex. It is based on "criteria relating to health and the perceptions of both the carer and the cared for. Nurses, like teachers, sometimes confuse the intention with the achievement" (p. 1555).

The Theory of Nursing as Caring

The theory of Nursing as Caring is a general (or grand) nursing theory that can be used as a framework to guide nursing practice. Framing the theory are several key assumptions:

- Persons are caring by virtue of their humanness.
- Persons live their caring from moment to moment.
- Persons are whole or complete in the moment.
- Personhood is living grounded in caring.
- Personhood is enhanced through participating in nurturing relationships with caring others.
- Nursing is both a discipline and a profession.

The most basic premise of the theory is that all humans are caring persons, that to be human is to be called to live one's innate caring nature. Developing the full potential of expressing caring is an ideal and is, for practical purposes, a lifelong process.

Grounded in these assumptions, the theory of nursing as caring posits the focus and the aim of nursing as a discipline of knowledge and a professional service with nurturing persons who live and grow in caring (Boykin

& Schoenhofer, 2001). When entering into a human-care situation the nurse focuses on coming to know the other as caring person, understanding how that person is living uniquely in the moment and living dreams and aspirations in caring. The aim of the nurse is to come to know and then affirm, support, and celebrate human beings as caring persons. Nursing is accomplished through acting on the informed intention to care in creative ways that are personally and situationally meaningful.

> An important concept in the theory of nursing as caring is that of nursing situation, understood to mean a shared, lived experience in which the caring between nurse and nursed enhances personhood.

An important concept in the theory of nursing as caring is that of the nursing situation. It is the shared, lived experience in which the caring between nurse and nursed enhances personhood (Boykin & Schoenhofer, 2001). Nursing situation is the context and the medium within which all nursing is created and expressed.

As the nurse enters into the world of the other with the intention of nurturing the person as caring, *calls for nursing* are heard. Calls for nursing originate within the nursed and are calls for nurturance through personal expressions of caring. In presence and intentionality, the nurse responds to these unique calls for nursing. Nursing responses are created in the moment as expressions of caring.

Coming to know the other as unique person, as a caring person, and responding with effective expressions of caring requires expertise on the part of the nurse. The expertise of the nurse is expertise in nursing-expertise in recognizing calls for caring in the other, in understanding how the other expresses personal dreams and aspirations for growing in caring, and in creating ways of caring in the moment that are truly nurturing. Mayeroff (1972) includes knowing, alternating rhythm, courage, hope, humility, trust, and patience as ingredients of caring, while Roach's (1987) six "C's" include the attributes of caring including compassion, conscience, competence, confidence, commitment, and comportment.

Practicing nursing from the conceptual and ethical perspective of the theory of nursing as caring means that the nurse need not judge self or other, neither weigh nor evaluate the amount of caring or the breakdown of caring—the nurse assumes from the beginning that the person *is* caring and acts accordingly. A well-formed intention and an authentic presence guide the nurse in selecting and organizing empirically-based knowledge for practical use in each unique and unfolding nursing situation. Nursing, then, is a service that is directed toward who the person is rather than who the person is not, and performs a unique function in the overall healthcare arena.

Technologies and Caring in Nursing

Machine technologies and caring in nursing can be harmonious aspects of clinical nursing practice. Often, the perception of technology and caring as dichotomous is so pervasive that one who is technologically proficient is assumed incapable of expressing caring. True technologic competence in clinical nursing practice can be understood as an expression of caring. It is in technological competency that knowing persons as whole or complete in the moment can be appreciated as a process of nursing. Technological competency assumes an indispensable place in contemporary clinical nursing practice.

Because of the prominence of medical and machine technology, patient care is frequently based on procedures that prolong patients' lives but that do not fully meet their need for care. Many encounters with patients seem to involve complex equipment and technologies that nurses monitor and document. Oftentimes, how well patients recover

> Because of the prominence of medical and machine technology, patient care is frequently based on procedures that prolong patients' lives but that do not fully meet their need for care.

determines patient satisfaction, which is often associated with the competent management of machinery. As all health professionals are well aware, dependence on machine technology is an indispensable ingredient of contemporary healthcare.

Personal Thoughts

Current concerns about nursing care as dependent upon expert utilization of machine technology was vividly described to me by a student who discussed a colleague's apprehension about the quality of nursing practice in an intensive care unit. Her colleague, a professional nurse, claimed that nursing routines in the unit had become so overwhelmingly machine-oriented, that she could no longer care for her patients. Most activities were centered on ventilators and cardiac monitors or documentation requirements that she believed prevented her from being caring. In her view, talking to patients and families was often considered superfluous, and seldom viewed as a nursing priority. She observed that such caring activities are often considered actions that require nursing time but ones with no immediate identifiable outcome. Nursing time spent being with a patient that does not show influence on expected patient outcomes is therefore considered expendable by some.

> For some, competence with machines and equipment in technologically demanding environments is the ultimate expression of caring in nursing and technologic incompetence is tantamount to not caring.

Machine technology can bring a patient closer to nurses because it enhances their knowledge of the person being cared for. Nonetheless, such technology may also widen the gap between a nurse and a patient because of an unconscious disregard of the patient as a person. While machine technology becomes a familiar work world for nurses, it may contribute to the alienation of patients for whom such a world is unfamiliar (Cooper, 1993).

Descriptions of the Technology-Caring Dichotomy in Nursing

The competent use of machine technology as integral to caring has been advanced by several scholars of nursing including Cooper (1993), Jones and Alexander (1993), Ray (1987), Sandelowski (1993), and Locsin (1995, 1998, 2001). Neighbors and Eldred (1993) emphasize that nurses must be able to address the complexity of nursing and develop technologic skills to keep pace with the rapid development of new technologies in healthcare. For some, competence with machines and equipment in technologically demanding environments is the ultimate expression of caring in nursing and technologic incompetence is tantamount to not caring.

Nurse scholars and practitioners are constantly searching for useful ways to understand and improve the practice of nursing. As has been noted, Boykin's and Schoenhofer's (2001) general theory of nursing as caring grounds the model of technological competency as caring in nursing. They posit that nursing occurs within nursing situations. These situations are the shared, lived experiences between nurse and the person being nursed. Within this nursing situation, the nurse hears, expresses, and addresses the *calls for nursing*. In like manner, the patient also seeks to be known and affirmed as a caring person. In a nursing situation, the nurse enters the world of the other with the intention of knowing the other as a caring person. Nursing responses are specific forms of caring created within a unique situation. In the caring process, each person grows in competency including technologic competency to express herself or himself as a caring person. Cooper (1993) states that machines and equipment are designed to be invulnerable, objective, and predictable. These features stand in contrast to the human characteristics of vulnerability, subjectivity, and unpredictability.

> " Cooper states that machines and equipment are designed to be invulnerable, objective, and predictable. These features stand in contrast to the human characteristics of vulnerability, subjectivity, and unpredictability. "

Professional nurses are challenged to be technologically competent while simultaneously recognizing human vulnerability when responding authentically and intentionally to calls for nursing. Authenticity and intentionality are demonstrated when a nurse appropriately accepts the patient's care as requiring high levels of technical expertise. In doing so, the nurse focuses her or his activities toward knowing the person fully as a caring human being who is in the process of living her or his hopes, dreams, and aspirations. Burfitt and colleagues (1993) describe caring for critically ill patients as a mutual process in which intentions from the nurse and patient are joined to form a shared experience.

> The competent exhibition of technology as caring is perceived as nursing practice if grounded on a perspective of nursing; otherwise, it is simply the practice of technological proficiency.

Technologic competence requires intentionality and authenticity, (Boykin and Schoenhofer, 2001), along with compassion, confidence, commitment, and conscience (Roach, 1987). Figure 5.1 shows three circles, one for each of the concepts: technologies and caring, technological competency, and nursing as caring. Boykin and Schoenhofer (1993) best explain the use of the circle as illustrating the commitment of people toward knowing self and others. The inner circle shows that the core concepts of technology and caring exist inseparably but relate distinctly as independent entities. The straight line dividing the circle into two distinct halves—and simultaneously demonstrating interconnectedness within the circle—represents this independence. Although the two core concepts are proximal and connected, they do not express the fullness of nursing.

The competent exhibition of technology as caring is perceived as nursing practice if grounded on a perspective of nursing; otherwise, it is simply the practice of technological proficiency.

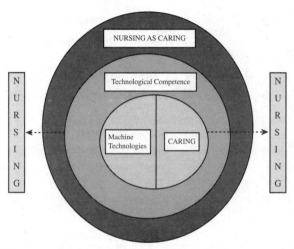

Figure 4.1 *The circles illustrate the commitment of people toward knowing self and others. The inner circle shows that the core concepts of technology and caring exist inseparably but relate distinctly as independent entities. The straight line dividing the circle into two distinct halves—and simultaneously demonstrating interconnectedness within the circle— represents this independence. Although the two core concepts are proximal and connected, they do not express the fullness of nursing.*

As people involved in giving care know, there are various ways of expressing caring. Professional nurses will continue to find meaning in their technological caring competencies and to express intentional and authentic presence in order to know the other as a whole person. Through the harmonious coexistence of technology and caring in the practice of nursing, the latter is transformed into a nursing-caring experience. Professionals and patients alike can only be grateful for the vast advances in medical and machine technology; however, their inclusion must not compromise the caring of nurses. As nursing professionals become more and more technically adept, they will find new and improved ways to build strong connections with patients through a practice of nursing using technologies competently in order to better know persons who are whole or complete in the moment.

> "Professional nurses will continue to find meaning in their technological caring competencies and to express intentional and authentic presence in order to know the other as a whole person."

Proficiency in technologies demonstrated without grounding in a nursing perspective is simply technological competency. When this occurs, people are not perceived as human beings who are complete in the moment and who therefore do not need to be fixed (Boykin and Schoenhofer, 2001). This is the dilemma of technology demonstrated as technologic competence without the benefit of a perspective of nursing—the perspective of caring.

References

Boykin, A., & Schoenhofer, S. (2001). *Nursing as caring: A model for transforming practice*. New York: Jones & Bartlett, National League for Nursing Press.

Deary, V., Deary, I., McKenna, H., McCance, T., Watson, R., & Hoogbruin, A. (2002). Elisions in the field of caring. *Journal of Advanced Nursing, 39*(1), 96-102.

Edwards, S. (2001). Benner and Wrubel on caring in nursing. *Journal of Advanced Nursing, 33*(2), 167-171.

Leininger, M. (Ed). (1988). Care: The essence of nursing and health. Thoroughfare, NJ: Slack.

Locsin, R. (1995). Machine technologies and caring in nursing. *Image: Journal of Nursing Scholarship, 27*(3), 201-203.

Locsin, R. (1998). Technologic competence as caring in critical care nursing. *Holistic Nursing Practice, 12*(4), 50-56.

Locsin, R. (2001). Practicing nursing: Technological competency as expression of caring in nursing. In R. Locsin (Ed.), Advancing technology, caring, and nursing. Westport, CT: Auburn House.

Lynaugh, J., & Fagin, C. (1988). Nursing comes of age. *Image: Journal of Nursing Scholarship, 20*(4), 184.

Mayeroff, M. (1972). *On caring*. New York: Harper Perennial.

Olson, T. (1993). Laying claim to caring: Nursing and the language of training, 1915-1937. *Nursing Outlook, 41*(2), 68-72.

Paley, J. (2001). An archeology of caring knowledge. *Journal of Advanced Nursing, 36*(2), 188-198.

Phillips, P. (1993). A deconstruction of caring. *Journal of Advanced Nursing, 18*, 1554-1558.

Ray, M. (1987). Technological caring: A new model in critical care. *Dimensions of Critical Care Nursing, 6*(3), 169-173

Roach, S. (1987). The human act of caring. Ottawa, Canada: Canadian Hospital Association.

Swanson, K. (1993). Nursing as informed caring for the well-being of others. *Image: Journal of Nursing Scholarship, 25*, 352-357.

Watson, J. (1985). *Nursing: The philosophy and science of caring.* Boulder, CO: Colorado Associated University Press.

"Understanding technological competency as having humanistic implications and meaning, and realizing that caring in various settings is expressed through all nursing activities, even those that are technological activities, makes this harmonious unification possible."

5

CHAPTER

Technological Competency as an Expression of Caring in Nursing

By Rozzano C. Locsin

The traditional question about the ontology of nursing reflects the growth of nursing as a knowledge and a practice profession. Its seeming constancy as a question is often ascribed to the perennial use of the word "nurse" referring to the performance of tasks, and as a consequence of the persisting image of nursing practice as the performing of tasks. The creation of the robo-nurse—a complex piece of machinery that, in human fashion, is made to perform technical nurse activities such as taking a person's temperature (Gutierrez, 2000)—perpetuates this image. The robo-nurse simply facilitates completion of tasks for people. The persistent image of nursing as accomplishing tasks undeniably makes the nurse appear to be an automaton (Locsin, 2001).

The advent of medical technology and its domination as the major influence in healthcare places nursing in an awkward position of being dependent upon competencies for these technologies in order to engage in practice. The practice of nursing as technological competency—an expression of caring in nursing—is the achievement of knowing persons as whole moment to moment. It is the authentic, intentional, knowledgeable, and efficient use of technologies of nursing. These technologies influence the recognition of nursing as integral to healthcare. As such, it recognizes the role technology has on the practice of nursing. Technological competency allows the nurse to participate in the process of knowing persons as whole in the moment. The ultimate purpose of technological competency is to continuously acknowledge persons as whole. Such acknowledgment compels the redesigning of processes of nursing—ways of expressing, celebrating, and appreciating the practice of nursing as continuously knowing persons as whole moment to moment. In this practice of nursing, technology is used not to know "what is the person?" but rather to know "who is the person?" While the former question alludes to the notion of persons as objects, the latter addresses the uniqueness and individuality of persons as human beings.

Description of Nursing Practice

Gadamer (1991) explains that "a practice is concerned not only with how to bring about the good, but what good or value is worth pursuing" (p. 83). In knowing persons wholeness through technology, this practice of nursing provides the opportunity for the nurse to continuously determine the fullness of the person as a human being.

The American Nurses Association (ANA) Code of Ethics for Nurses (2000) describes nursing practice as focusing on the achievement of promoting health and preventing illness. While this may be the ideal, nurses in their preferred practice arenas may not be provided with many such opportunities. Contemporary practice settings often preferred by nurses are intensive and critical care units where the desired qualification is technological competency. However, with the prevailing re-envisioning of health system policies, expectations of technological competencies are also desired and required in non-intensive or non-critical care arenas. While it is necessary to understand the operation of machine devices in order to understand the functioning human being, the use of these technologies should not consign persons to be regarded as objects. The objectification of persons becomes an ordinary occurrence in situations wherein the practice of nursing is merely understood as achievement of tasks.

> "The ANA Code of Ethics for Nurses (2000) describes nursing practice as focusing on the achievement of promoting health and preventing illness. While this may be the ideal, nurses in their preferred practice arenas may not be provided with many such opportunities."

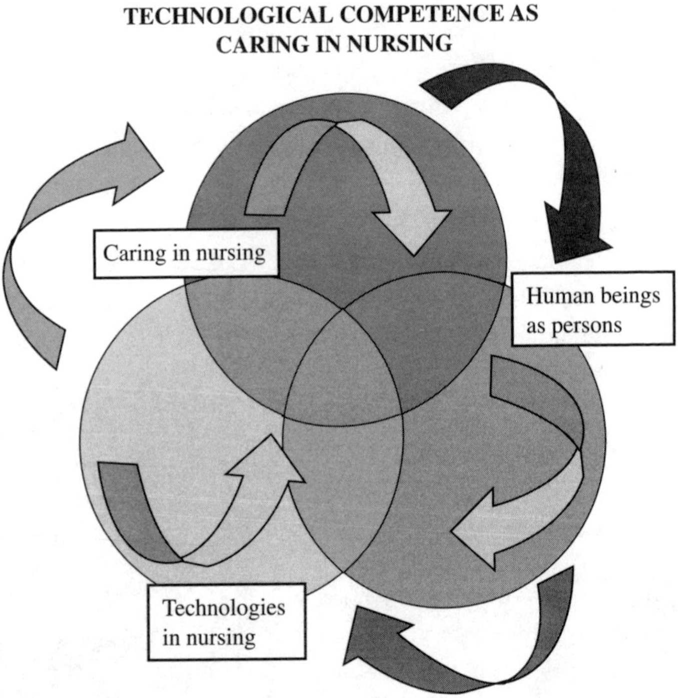

TECHNOLOGICAL COMPETENCE AS CARING IN NURSING

Figure 5.1   *Multidirectional arrows signify motions indicating on-going advancement and continuous revelations of information achieved through technologies in nursing, all about human beings who are whole, dynamic, and unpredictable. Expanding technologies in nursing are ever-changing, and ceaselessly demanding, while caring in nursing is the substantive body of knowledge that drives the practice of knowing persons as whole and integrating technological competency as nursing. These critical components in the overall concept of technological competency as caring in nursing are represented by the outer arrows moving inward and outward in many directions indicating the process of nursing as repetitive, decreasing possibilities for objectification. Technological competence as caring in nursing is a process illustrated as movements indicating the dynamic, responding, and continuous process of knowing persons as whole in the moment.*

Technological Competency as Expression of Caring in Nursing

To professional nurses, activities involving machine technologies such as monitoring ventilators and EKGs create overwhelming demands on being competent with technologies. Activities such as interpreting data from cardiac monitors, manipulating ventilators and intravenous pumps, or even the skill of starting intravenous lines are frequently recognized as demonstrations of technological competency rather than as expressions of caring in nursing. In situations where technologies are used to know "what is" the patient rather than "who is" the patient (see figure 5.1), the authentic intention to know persons as whole in the moment is often devalued (Locsin, 1998).

Subservience with Technology

Intensive care units (ICU) emerged in the 1950s as a technologic system of tools, knowledge, and skills to care for critically ill patients. The few historical studies of the ICU neglect nursing care, rendering nurse's work invisible and unacknowledged. Past studies focus on machines and physicians even though nursing is what is intensive about ICUs. During the initiation of critical care units, nurses' traditional practices of intensive observation and triage provided the model for the care of the critically ill in ICUs. Importantly, nurses sought out the knowledge needed to care for critically ill patients in order to supplement traditional practices. In doing so, nurses gained greater expertise in valuing their work environment and their patient care (Fairman, 1992).

> "During the initiation of critical care units, nurses' traditional practices of intensive observation and triage provided the model for the care of the critically ill in ICUs."

The establishment of ICUs was a response to the demands of the increasing severity and acuity of patient conditions. These patient conditions were results of advancing technologies—motorized vehicles and other high technology tools like war implements and automatic guns—such as the Thompson machine gun that delivers multiple bullets in one pull of the trigger or the shotgun that can inflict multiple wounds in one shot—which increased the mortality and morbidity rates of people. These high tech gunshot injuries were frequently to the more delicate organs of the body such as the lungs or the brain, and the vehicular accidents caused frequent head and musculo-skeletal injuries.

The practice of nursing in the 21st century is typified by expressions of technological competency. Grounding such a practice on the perspective of Nursing as Caring (Boykin and Schoenhofer, 2001) allows for the celebration of persons in their wholeness. Because the practice of nursing is dominated by technology, caring in nursing is simultaneously revealed to be the harmonious coexistence between technology and caring (Locsin 1995). In today's healthcare structure, the major characteristic desired of healthcare personnel is technological proficiency. Patient satisfaction usually focuses on how well recovery was facilitated by the nurse, which for the most part is associated with competency in using machine technologies (Locsin, 1995).

> "To some nurses, activities that are technology-based often seem uncaring, but to technology-competent nurses, these are normal activities reflecting nursing in critical settings"

Often, nursing practitioners declare that the demands of technological competency in technology-dependent settings are so arduous that caring is no longer possible. In this association, "caring" usually means activities performed with the patient, such as holding the patient's hand or being physically present and interacting. These activities are empirical examples of the nature of being with the patient from the traditional view of a caring nurse. While being with the patient may be an expression of a feeling, caring nurse, many perceive this caring nursing practice as time spent or wasted, and actions undertaken that do not influence the health of patients, and which therefore, are expendable. To some nurses, activities that are technology-based often seem uncaring, but to technology-competent nurses, these are normal activities reflecting nursing in critical settings.

Technology and Competency in Nursing

Technology comprises methods and expressions that delineate structures and procedures in techniques. *Technique* is a standard procedure that can be taught—a recipe that can be duplicated and that when followed always leads to the desired end. In nursing, technology is expressed in procedures facilitating nursing activities. Technique is exemplified by the nursing process—a recipe that when followed illustrates the mechanistic view of nursing practice.

The level of knowledge the nurse possesses does not afford the whole understanding of the person as the focus of nursing. Instead, with the intentional and authentic presence (Paterson & Zderad, 1988) brought into the situation, the nurse may be able to know the other fully as a person living unique hopes, dreams, and aspirations. Nursing technologies that are enacted for the sole purpose of procedural efficiency only sustain the impression that nursing practice is simply technological proficiency (Locsin, 1998).

Competency is recognized and advocated as an effective component of technology in nursing practice (Girot, 1993; Miller, Hoggan, Pringle & West, 1993). The rapid development of technology and its increased utility in healthcare have contributed to this phenomenon. Miller, et al (1993), ascribe two meanings to competence:

- Competence equated with performance and referred to descriptively as an activity, and
- Competence as a quality or state of being of an individual.

In the former meaning, competence is easily envisioned as the product, while the latter meaning exhibits a characteristic of one who performs the activity. These attributes highlight the description of competency as meaningful and distinctive to the practice of nursing (Miller, et al, (1993). Expert nurses use these meanings intuitively in providing care and in using theory in their practice (Benner, 1984).

Competency with Technology as Practice of Nursing

The pressure to achieve technological proficiency in nursing practice has inspired re-visioning of the technology-caring dichotomy (Locsin, 1995). Beginning in the 1970s with the nursing dialogue centered on care versus cure, research in nursing has since focused on nursing knowledge development, with nursing practice as the focal arena. The prominence that caring has gained as a central expression of nursing is evidence of this emphasis. Current importance ascribed to technology is a sign of the successful incorporation of technological competency as caring in nursing.

Technology has the potential to bring the patient closer to the nurse by enhancing the nurse's ability to know more about the person. Conversely, technology can also increase the gap between the nurse and client as exhibited by the conscious disregard of the patient as "person," and ignorance of the nursing imperative to know the patient as "person." Technology defines a familiar work world for the nurse, but it also can contribute to the alienation of the patient (Porter, 1992).

Technological Competency as Caring

Concepts implicit in the theory of nursing as caring (Boykin & Schoenhofer, 2001), ground the understanding of technological competency as caring in nursing—a way in which technology and caring are unified in the practice of nursing. A nurse who is technologically proficient but does not know the patient fully as a person in the moment is the ultimate example of one who is simply a technologist (Locsin, 1995). Understanding technological competency as having humanistic implications and meaning, and realizing that caring in various settings is expressed through all nursing activities, even those that are technological activities, makes this harmonious unification possible (Locsin 1998).

Persons grow in their competency to express themselves as caring persons (Boykin & Schoenhofer, 2001). This competency may well be conceived as the nurse's caring demonstrated as technological competency while being authentically present with the patient. To appreciate technological competency as caring, its use as a means to an end and as a human activity must reflect intention-to-nurse and technological responsibility. It is in this context that the nurse is challenged to care.

> The nurse understands that the process of nursing occurs without preconceived views that categorize persons as needing to be fixed, like fitting the individuals into boxes of predicted conditions.

Nursing in a Technological Environment

Technological competency as caring involves intentionality with compassion, confidence, commitment, and conscience as requisites to caring in nursing. This is where the process of nursing takes on a focus different from the traditional series of problem-solving actions. By donning the lens of Nursing as Caring (Boykin & Schoenhofer, 2001), technological competency as caring in nursing is acknowledged. Through this lens, nursing is expressed as the simultaneous, momentary interconnectedness between the nurse and the nursed (Locsin, 1995). The nurse relies on the patient for calls for nursing. These calls are specific mechanisms that patients use, and they provide the opportunity for the nurse to respond with the authentic intention to know the other fully as a whole and complete person. Calls for nursing may be expressed as hopes, dreams, and aspirations. As uniquely as these nursing situations are expressed, the nurse is challenged to hear these calls for nursing and to respond authentically and intentionally in nurturance. These appropriate responses may be communicated as patterns of relating information, such as those derived from machines like the EKG monitor, in order to know the physiological status of the person in the moment, or to administer life-saving medications, institute transfers, or to refer patients to other healthcare professionals as an advocate for the patient in the moment.

The challenge of nursing is expressing technological competency as caring, ably focusing on the other as caring person, whole and complete in the moment, and growing in caring from moment to moment. Every human being uniquely responds to personal conditions in the moment. The nurse understands that the process of nursing occurs without preconceived views that categorize persons as needing to be fixed, like fitting the individuals into boxes of predicted conditions. By allowing the patient to unfold as a person and to live fully as a human being, the nurse facilitates the goal of nursing in the "caring between" and enhances personhood of both the nursed and the nurse (Boykin and Schoenhofer, 2001).

Nursing practitioners long for a practice of nursing that is based on the authentic desire to know persons fully as human beings rather than as objects. Through this authentic intention and desire, nurses are challenged to use every creative, imaginative, and innovative way possible to appreciate and celebrate the person's intentions to live more fully and grow as a human being. Only with expertise with technologies of nursing can technological competence as an expression of caring in nursing be realized. Describing nursing practice as the completion of tasks does not serve the profession well. Nurses are urged to value technological competency as an expression of caring in nursing and as integral to healthcare. Otherwise, the image of the robo-nurse, simply facilitating completion of tasks for people, undeniably will make a nurse an automaton.

> *Describing nursing practice as the completion of tasks does not serve the profession well.*

References

American Nurses Association. (2000). *Code of ethics*. Washington, DC: Author.

Benner, P. (1984). *From novice to expert*. Menlo Park, CA: Addison-Wesley.

Boykin, A., & Schoenhofer, S. (2001). *Nursing as caring: A model for transforming practice*. New York: Jones & Bartlett, National League for Nursing Press.

Fairman, J. (1992). Watchful vigilance: Nursing care, technology, and the development of intensive care units. *Nursing Research, 41*(1), 56-60.

Girot, E. (1993). Assessment of competence in clinical practice: A phenomenological approach. *Journal of Advanced Nursing, 8*, 114-119.

Gutierrez, L. (2000, March 1). Robo nurse? *Palm Beach Post*, 3D.

Porter, S. (1992). The poverty of professionalization: A critical analysis of strategies for the occupational advancement of nursing. *Journal of Advanced Nursing, 17*, 723-728.

Locsin, R. (1995). Machine technologies and caring in nursing. *Image: Journal of Nursing Scholarship, 27*(3), 201-203.

Locsin, R. (1998). Technologic competence as expression of caring in nursing. *Holistic Nursing Practice, 12*(4), 50-56.

Locsin, R. (2001) The culture of technology: Defining transformation in nursing from "The Lady with a Lamp" to "Robonurse"? *Holistic Nursing Practice, 16*(1), 1-4.

Miller, C., Hoggan, J., Pringle, S., & West, G. (1993). Credit where credit is due. The report of the accreditation of work based learning Project, 1988. *Journal of Advanced Nursing, 8*, 114-119.

Paterson, J., & Zderad, P. (1988). *Humanistic nursing*. New York: National League for Nursing Press.

2

PART

Practice Issues

"If technology is the practice of applying scientific knowledge, and if the focus of nursing, as a human science, is caring, then the technology of caring can also be regarded as the practical application of human science."

6

CHAPTER

Technology of Caring: A Practical Application of Nursing

By Rozzano C. Locsin

In the early- to mid-1990s, the idea of technology and caring in nursing as dichotomous was furthered and popularized. Nowhere was this popularity as honored as in nursing practice. Concerned with the professionalization of nursing and with providing evidence on knowledge-based practice, nurses believed that in order for nursing to be a profession and to be valued as an integral factor in the attainment and maintenance of health, it was essential that nurses be technologically adept and clinically competent.

Today, the contention that technology and caring exist concurrently in nursing is becoming recognized. In a 1995 germinal work concerning machine technologies and caring in nursing, Locsin declared the harmonious coexistence of technology and caring, and the model of technological competency as caring was born. The article spurred exhaustive debate among scholars of nursing. The debates stimulated and motivated scholarly investigations into the coexistence of technology and caring in nursing.

- What spawned the thinking of congruency between technology and caring in nursing?
- How was congruency "expressed" in the articulation of the model?

These questions legitimize the purpose of this chapter which are to describe and explain the coexistence between technology and caring in nursing, to explain the framework through which the coexistence is viewed, and to appreciate the fullness of nursing in the unfolding of a perspective of caring expressed through competency with technologies in nursing.

> "The perception of technology and caring as a dichotomy is so pervasive that someone who is technologically proficient is often assumed to be less capable of expressing caring."

Central to the struggle of explaining the framework of the coexistence between technology and caring in nursing is the attempt to realize that caring in nursing is "a mutual human process in which the nurse, recognizing *self* and *other* as caring person, responds with authentic presence to specific calls for nursing" (Boykin and Schoenhofer, 2001, p. 23). The perception of technology and caring as a dichotomy is so pervasive that someone who is technologically proficient is often assumed to be less capable of expressing caring. While technology is the passion to be mechanistic and practical in the application of science, caring is the pre-occupation to be compassionate and humanistic in support of human consciousness (Ray, 1987). If technology is the practice of applying scientific knowledge, and if the focus of nursing, as a human science, is caring, then the technology of caring can also be regarded as the practical application of human science. Within an emerging framework of technological competency as caring in nursing expressed through knowing persons continuously moment to moment, true technological competence as nursing practice is understood as an expression of caring.

Technology, competency, and caring are concepts that have gained public notice as illustrated by recent nursing literature and a recently concluded international nursing conference on "Nursing in a Technological World" in Brisbane, Australia. Representatives from 20 countries worldwide came to the conference, underscoring of the richness of technology in nursing as an area of scholarly investigation.

The identification of technology and caring as simultaneously existing in nursing practice focuses the meaning of technological caring as "the experience of caring [that] comes as a process of growth [where] technical achievement is one of the meanings" (Ray, 1987, p. 170). Technology and competence enhance effective caring, yet it is being observed that technology also impedes care by alienating and dehumanizing both the nurse and the patient, particularly when technological competence is not skillfully blended with sensitivity to the needs and responses of the patient. Objectification of persons is critical. It maintains the idea that persons are objects that are to be known in order for the practice of prescriptive and predictive nursing to take place. A perspective of practice such as this perpetuates this understanding.

As an expression of caring, technological competency assumes an indispensable place in contemporary nursing practice. The explorations of the meaning of technology, caring, competence, and nursing are integral to the appreciation of technological competency as a practical application of human science.

> 66 Technology and competence enhance effective caring, yet it is being observed that technology also impedes care by alienating and dehumanizing both the nurse and the patient, particularly when technological competence is not skillfully blended with sensitivity to the needs and responses of the patient. 99

The belief that life that is artificially supported by machine technology is unnatural predominates discussions among practitioners of nursing, particularly when the subject of concern is technology dependency in healthcare. As long as the person is perceived as object, the debate regarding technology in nursing practice—often perceived as the practice of using machine-dependent support—continues to uphold the misconception that this dichotomy between technology and caring in nursing influences the critical nature of nursing healthcare. Technological competence in nursing is not antithetical to the practice of nursing as caring, but rather is an expression of its influence. As such, its coexistence with nursing enhances the realization of its position within the domain of nursing practice. Central to this consciousness is the view that persons are not human bodies identified only as objects, but rather they are individuals who possess values of dignity and autonomy and who strive to live their hopes, dreams, and aspirations as persons.

In describing the evolution of the definition of "high-tech" nursing care, Casetta (1993a, 1993b) described the practice as nursing for technology-dependent patients who require intensive support in specialized units like critical care areas. High-tech nurses, therefore, are achievement-oriented practitioners with a level of competence that complies with the advanced nature of technology within the area of practice, thus allowing a more expeditious way of processing interventions for the patients who are dependent on specialized technology. Today, however, the setting of high-tech nursing has spread into traditionally non-high-tech arenas. The consequent demand for technological caring and the re-orientation of nursing practice is more greatly felt. High-tech nursing is the epitome of technology-dependent nursing, a versatility of nursing practice that is both a blessing and a curse for nursing as a discipline and a profession. A blessing because it increases the value of nursing from a social-need perspective and a curse because oftentimes it limits the perception of nursing practice as simply competency with technology, making nursing practitioners technologists. The conception of technological competency as an expression of caring in nursing informs a practice of nursing as more than technological expertise—it fosters the value of competency with technology as an expertise of practice generated from a science-based, knowledgeable, and compassionate practice.

> "Central to this consciousness is the view that persons are not human bodies identified only as objects, but rather they are individuals who possess values of dignity and autonomy and who strive to live their hopes, dreams, and aspirations as persons."

Ethical decisions in high-tech nursing focus on issues about the quality of a patient's life with or without technological support. Nurses are in a position to make assessments about the best course of action for each individual because of the time they spend with patients (Casetta, 1993). While some professional nurses are more comfortable with technology, all nurses must advocate for a balance between working with technology and providing hands-on nursing. Certainly, nurses must remain in touch with the advances in nursing and healthcare technologies, however, not to the extent of abandoning human responses as compassionate expressions of care (Peck, 1992). Apparently, situations in which advanced technology can distance nurses from patients (because they need to pay attention to the equipment) exist. With the information derived from equipment, critical information can be retrieved that allows nurses to focus on care while being in relationship with the person (Hudson, 1988).

> With the information derived from equipment, critical information can be retrieved which allows nurses to focus on caring while being in relationship with the person (Hudson, 1988).

While technological competence is expressed as technical achievement in practice, being supportive and expressive—as one of the ways in which care is demonstrated—enhances the humanness of technological proficiency. Being technologically proficient is recognized as the expressive/supportive exhibition of nursing as demonstrated through care. When technology is used to know persons continuously, moment-to-moment, the process of nursing is lived.

Describing Technology in Nursing

Technology, in relation to the practice of nursing, is viewed as a means to an end and as a human activity (Heidegger, 1977). As a means to an end, activities like *procuring* and *utilizing* indicate a process driven by human activity. Within this framework is *instrumentality*. It is considered fundamental to the characteristic of technology that every attempt should be made by the utilizer to bring human beings into the right relation to technology. "Everything depends on manipulating technology in the proper manner as means" (Heidegger, 1977, pp. 6). When nursing activities influence the patient's well-being, the description of technology as a means to an end, a human activity, and as instrument is exacting.

Technologies in nursing are perceived in various ways including computer literacy and robotic proficiency that allow nurses to know and assist the patient more fully towards well-being (Peck, 1992). Computers and other healthcare technology have the potential to interfere with nurses' decisions and abilities to confirm patients as persons. It also has the potential to divert nurses away from providing care that is personally confirming to patients (Menix, 1993). As exemplified in the process of rehabilitation, Platts and Frase (1993) likened technology to the skillful manipulation of assistive functions for patients, particularly on mobility (wheelchairs and cars), functionality (page-turning, robotic arms), communication (keyboard emulators, voice processors) and control of the environment (automatons, sensorimeters, and nanotechnologies). Hudson (1993) alludes to technology as "curing," emphasizing technological and physical competence, while Reilly and Behrens-Hanna (1991) refer to technology as that which addresses moral and ethical issues inherent in the practice of nursing. The sophisticated technological advancement towards the achievement of quality patient care is certain among patients. The valuing that exists between technology and clinical evaluations was presented by Pierson and Funk (1989) who found that data made available by a pulmonary artery catheter were in no instance identified as factors used to determine fluid management decisions; rather, data obtained by non-invasive clinical evaluations like urine output, chest x-ray, and edema were used. This leads us to express concerns about the legitimacy of various technologies that are used on patients. The impact of technology in nursing practice is very well demonstrated in Cooper's (1993) consecration of the intensive care unit as the ultimate place where technology is experienced, in that "nowhere is the nature of technology more evident than in the micro culture of an intensive care unit. This is where the dominance of technology renders many experiences invisible. ICU's are inescapably distinguished and defined by technology" (p. 24). Hudson (1993) described the situation as the ultimate environment for technologically-proficient nurses, which further explains the delineation between empathy as caring and technology as curing in the coronary care unit. Hudson further claims that because of the technology expertise demanded of the nurse in the coronary care units and the cure-oriented focus, the specialty has also become especially attractive to male nurses.

In 2001, Alexander and Kroposki proposed to clearly define nursing technology. In reviewing the literature, they found that the concept of technology in nursing is variably used. From the perspectives and descriptions of nurse managers, they studied definitions of nursing technology from managers' perspectives at a distance of ten years apart. The findings suggest that the dimensions of nursing technology change over time and support the need for nurse managers to periodically assess nursing technology before making management changes at the level of the nursing unit. Common interpretations of technology in healthcare include devices such as EKG monitors, healthcare computers, imaging devices, and ventilators. Increasing concern about confusing appreciations of technology further enhances the need to clarify and put into context a common definition, or at the least, identify the commonality that exists among the uses of technology in nursing and healthcare. For example, there are varying descriptions of technology as techniques, equipment, and procedures that facilitate nursing actions (Locsin, 1995), or as a selection of processes and systems (Nagle, 1998) influential to nursing practice. Still, other descriptions of technologies used in nursing increase the confusion, such as reproductive technology, imaging monitoring technologies (Sandelowski, 1998), and assistive technologies enhancing true presence (Bernardo,1998; Simms & McHugh, 2000). Essentially, Alexander and Kroposki (2001) define nursing technology as "nursing care processes used to change the status of an individual from a patient to a person no longer requiring nursing care" (p. 778).

Barnard (1996) attempted to dissect the definition of technology and nursing. Although this work was not specifically to define technology as a phenomenon, issues were addressed pertaining to the formulation of a definition and the methods nurses used to understand technology in their practices. Describing the three layers of meaning of technology, Barnard succinctly contextualized the use of technology in nursing practice:

- The first layer meaning addresses the instrumental aspect of technology, as in machines and tools.
- The second layer meaning addresses technology as knowledge, which includes an appreciation of the instrument and the expertise subsequent to it.

- The third layer of meaning addresses the understanding of technology as the creation of a technical phenomenon, wherein technique is appreciated as the bedrock from which technology is founded.

This third layer of technology encompasses a greater breadth of appreciation, forming a relative understanding of the world from the perspective of the two earlier meanings. Using these three layers of meaning, nurses are able to bring a clearer definition and description of nursing.

> The power of technology as means to an end and as a human activity was set, not because of equipment or the availability of instruments, but because of the intensity of the technology that was demanded to sustain and maintain human life.

An experienced nurse who said, "often times what people see are ICU nurses who are focusing a lot on machines because machines are giving tremendous bodily physical support to that patient," defends the intensive care unit as technology's definitive locale. The machines are actually fundamental for us in this kind of unit (Cooper, 1993, p. 26). Further support for this perception of the ICU nurse was noted as early as the 1950s. "The nurses did not consider familiar equipment and machines 'technology.' To them, technology represented 'new' science, machines (such as dialysis machines and heart monitors) that were complex and actually sustained patients or provided previously unobtainable data" (Fairman, 1992 p. 58.). The power of technology as means to an end and as a human activity was set, not because of equipment or the availability of instruments, but because of the intensity of the technology that was demanded to sustain and maintain human life. Competence in triage and the complexity of the observations that transpire 24 hours a day through the vigilance of nurses demonstrate this intensity in emergency and trauma situations as well as in critical care areas. Technical knowledge and capabilities do not easily translate into power and control (Reverby, 1987) thereby facilitating the coexistence of technology in nursing situations.

Familiar terms that tend to dilute the impact of nursing activities in healthcare are technique and technology. Zwolski (1989) describes technique as "simply a standard method that can be taught, a recipe that can be duplicated and if followed, it will lead to the desired end, whereas technology is the embodiment of technique" (p. 238). As such, it can be recognized by its methods and expressions as in reproductive technology which uses certain techniques like fetal monitoring, in vitro fertilization, and artificial insemination that are easily identified as aspects of reproduction technology (Zwolski, 1989).

> The question remains, what comprises unique nursing technologies?

Technology in nursing is important if it is to be understood as a human activity and as a means to attain the well-being of patients and the support of policymakers, third party payers, and other healthcare professionals and administrators (Jacox et al., 1990). The impact of healthcare reform, particularly on the subject of uniqueness of technology used in nursing practice, the autonomy of nurses, and ownership of such technologies have been described as critical to the contemporary value of the practice of nursing. From definitions of nursing to definitions of allied health professions, Jacox, et al, have exulted the need to classify those technologies that nurses use. Although ownership of a particular technology consistently instigates academic discussions between and amongst proponent owners, it is succinctly stressed that "if technology is used by more than one discipline, that technology is not owned by any single profession, nor can any single profession claim the sole right to be reimbursed for the technology"(p. 84). The question remains, what comprises unique nursing technologies? Technology in nursing brings the nurse in mutually-dependent encounters with the person being nursed, with the purpose to facilitate the living of each other's hopes, dreams, and aspirations. Therefore, the purpose of technology in nursing is not just to retrieve data, achieve particular status among healthcare providers, or to simply exhibit proficiency, but rather, and most importantly, to know intentionally the person fully as a whole and living person.

Currently, three theoretical perspectives that affect the study of technology and caring in nursing exist: Technological caring (Ray, 1987), technology dependency (Sandelowski, 1993), and technological competency as caring in nursing (Locsin, 1998).

Technological Caring

Ray (1994, personal communication) proposed the concept of technological caring during her early years of scientific work. Technological caring is described as the ethical process of believing in the power of technology to change or reverse the patient's state, influence nurses' decisions to allow patients to live or die peacefully with moral reasoning that focuses on obligations to "do no harm (beneficence and no maleficence), to be fair (justice), and to allow choice (autonomy)." (Ray, 1987, p. 167).

Because critical care nurses usually work to sustain life, these experiential ethical shifts are important while understanding more fully the meaning of caring. In order to do this, three operative processes were found: The dominant values of the critical care nurse who believed in technology and treatment,

> The purpose of technology in nursing is not just to retrieve data, achieve particular status among healthcare providers, or to simply exhibit proficiency, but rather, and most importantly, to know intentionally the person fully as a whole and living person.

how the uses of technology were interpreted, and the extent of patient suffering. While these processes operate on the ethical and moral aspects of reasoning in technological caring, compassion motivates the change "in the ethical decision-making process of technological caring . . . thus unity of meaning between the experience of critical care and technological caring has its foundation in ethics, in the coexistent relationship between experience and principle" (p. 170).

Technology Dependency

Sandelowski (1993) defined technology dependency as "that short- or long-term reliance on devices and techniques to evaluate or satisfy or resolve health-related needs or problems"(p. 37). *People* are described in reference to their involvement in the invention, dissemination, application, and use of technology, including such individuals as the recipients of healthcare services, nurses, physicians, technicians, and repair personnel. *Tools* include devices, instruments, and machines like thermometers, CT scanners, and sphygmomanometers. *Technique*, on the other hand, refers to the procedures that put tools to clinical use such as venipuncture, cardiac catheterization, and surgery. Sandelowski described the existence and unintended outcomes based on operations and intervening processes. While technology dependency is appreciated as existing in order to know the patients, it is similarly desired through the recognition and proposition of possible independence to technology, that reliance on non-technological means to evaluate or resolve health problems can be acknowledged.

Technological Competency as Caring

The perspective of technological competency as caring in nursing (Locsin, 1998) was derived from a germinal work in which it was proposed that technology and caring could exist harmoniously. Technological competency as caring in nursing describes its focus as knowing persons as whole and complete in the moment. All nursing takes place in nursing situations—those shared, lived experiences between the nurse and nursed. Mutual and continuous knowing of persons is expressed as the nurse intentionally and authentically knowing persons as whole in the moment, while likewise, the person or other allows the nurse to enter her or his world so that the nurse may know her or him as a whole person. Of important consideration is the other person's intention to know the nurse as a person as well. In order to appreciate technological competency as caring, its utilization as means to an end and as a human activity must be personified with evidences and proofs of intentionality (Purnell, 2003) and technological responsibility while being supported by a theoretical model of nursing. The professional nurse is challenged to be technologically masterful while responding authentically and intentionally to calls for nursing. This authenticity and intentionality are demonstrated when the nurse accepts the person and attempts to know the person fully as in the process of living her or his hopes, dreams, and aspirations.

Burfitt, et al (1993) succinctly described caring for critically ill persons as a "mutual process in which intentions are joined to form a shared experience. In this mutual process, healing is an outcome that might otherwise be elusive" (p. 489). This authenticity and intentionality are demonstrated when the nurse accepts the person and attempts to know the person fully as one who is in the process of living her or his hopes, dreams, and aspirations as a caring person.

> All nursing takes place in nursing situations—those shared, lived experiences between the nurse and nursed.

Summary

Considered independently, technology and caring reveal a discordant relationship. This is typically evident in activities of non-professional nurses who are regarded as the "equivalent of the lower orders in nursing and are being renamed care assistants, indicating differences of status between nursing and caring" (Phillips, 1993, p. 1557). This description of types of care givers perpetuates the effects of language and tends to dichotomize caring and technology while fostering its paradoxical existence. A nurse who performs technological proficiency without the knowledge of the person is the ultimate example of a nurse who is simply a technologist. How technology is defined (as having more humanistic meaning and as caring as more of an international interaction or therapeutic intervention), instigates the realization of the harmonious or discordant existence of technologies of caring as a practical application of nursing.

As Cooper (1993) argued, "technology is designed to be invincible, invulnerable, objective, and predictable, in contrast to the human characteristics of vulnerability, subjectivity, and unpredictability" (p. 26). It is in this context that the nurse is challenged to care.

Herein lies the paradoxical exhibition of technology and caring in nursing. Herein lies the power of caring technology that facilitates the viewing of persons as human beings, rather than as objects, who possess values of dignity and autonomy, who strive to live their hopes, dreams, and aspirations as whole persons. Technology of nursing is the practice application of caring in nursing.

References

Alexander, J., & Kroposki, M. (2001). Using a management perspective to define and measure changes in nursing technology. *Journal of Advanced Nursing, 35*(5), 776-783.

Barnard, A. (1996). Technology and nursing: An anatomy of definition. *International Journal of Nursing Studies, 33*(4). 433-441.

Bernardo, A. (1998). Technology and true presence. *Holistic Nursing Practice, 12*(4), 40-49.

Boykin, A., & Schoenhofer, S. (2001). *Nursing as caring: A model for transforming practice.* New York: Jones & Bartlett, National League for Nursing Press.

Burfitt, S., Greiner, D., Miers, L., Kinney, M., & Branyon, M. (1993). Professional nurse caring as perceived by critically ill patients: A phenomenologic study. *American Journal of Critical Care, 2*(6), 489-499.

Casetta, R. (1993a, November-December). The evolution of high-tech nursing. *The American Nurse,* 18-19.

Casetta, R. (1993b, November-December). Nurses advocate for ethical decisions in high-tech care. *The American Nurse,* 30.

Cooper, M. (1993). The intersection of technology and care in the ICU. *Advances in Nursing Science, 15*(3), 23-32.

Fairman, J. (1992). Watchful vigilance: Nursing care, technology, and the development of intensive care units. *Nursing Research, 41*(1), 56-60.

Hudson, R. (1988). Whole or parts–a theological perspective on "person." *The Australian Journal of Advanced Nursing, 6*(1), 12-20.

Hudson, G. (1993). Empathy and technology in the coronary care unit. *Intensive Critical Care Nursing, 9*(1), 55-61.

Heidegger, M. (1977). *The question concerning technology and other essays*. New York: Harper & Row.

Jacox, A., Pillar, B., & Redman, B. (1990). A classification of nursing technology. *Nursing Outlook, 38*(2), 81-85.

Locsin, R. (1995). Machine technologies and caring in nursing. *Image: Journal of Nursing Scholarship, 27*(3), 201-203.

Locsin, R (1998). Technologic competence as expression of caring in critical care settings. *Holistic Nursing Practice, 12*(4), 50-56.

Lynaugh, J., & Fagin, C. (1988). Nursing outcomes of age. *Image: Journal of Nursing Scholarship, 20*(4), 184.

Menix, K. (1993). Technology: Complementing or controlling care? *The International Nurse News and Views, 7*(1), 1-6.

Nagle, L.M. (1998). The meaning of technology for people with chronic renal failure. *Holistic Nursing Practice, 12*(4), 78-92.

Peck, M. (1992). The future of nursing in a technological age: Computers, robots, and TLC. *Journal of Holistic Nursing, 10*(2), 183-191.

Pierson, M., & Funk, M. (1989). Technology versus clinical evaluation for fluid management decisions in CABG patients. *Image: Journal of Nursing Scholarship, 21*(4), 192-195.

Phillips, P. (1993). A deconstruction of caring. *Journal of Advanced Nursing, 18*, 554-1558.

Purnell, M. (2003). *Intentionality in nursing*. Unpublished doctoral dissertation, University of Miami School of Nursing, Florida.

Ray, M. (1987). Technological caring: A new model in critical care. *Dimensions of Critical Care Nursing, 6*(3), 169-173.

Reverby, S. (1987). A caring dilemma: Womanhood and nursing in historical perspective. *Nursing Research, 36*(1), 5-11.

Reilly, D., & Behrens-Hanna, L. (1991). Perioperative nursing: Moral and ethical issues in high-technology practice. *Today's OR Nurse, 13*(8), 10-15.

Sandelowski, M. (1993). Toward a theory of technology dependency. *Nursing Outlook, 41*(1), 36-42.

Sandelowski, M. (1998) . Looking to care of caring to look? Technology and the rise of spectacular nursing. *Holistic Nursing Practice, 12*(4), 1-11.

Simms, L., & McHugh, M. (2000). Assistive technology. In L. Simms, S. Price, & N. Ervin (Eds.), *Professional practice of nursing administration* (3rd ed.; pp. 583-599). Albany, NY: Delmar.

Zwolski, K. (1989). Professional nursing in a technical system. *Image: Journal of Nursing Scholarship, 21*(4), 238-242.

> "For some, competence with machines and equipment in technologically demanding environments is the ultimate expression of caring in nursing and technologic incompetence is tantamount to not caring."

7

CHAPTER

A Model for Practice: Technological Competency as Caring in Nursing

By Rozzano C. Locsin

This chapter presents the foundational concepts of the model "technological competency as caring in nursing." As a model of professional practice that guides the process of nursing, technological competency as caring is the proficient use of technology for the singular purpose of knowing the person as whole and complete from moment to moment. Viewing persons as whole is critical to the appreciation of the contemporary practice of professional nursing. The ultimate concept is the understanding that nursing practice allows for the nurturance of persons, not for a process of fixing them because they are broken or to make them whole again because they are missing aspects of themselves.

In this model, nursing is described as "knowing" persons. Knowing is a continuous process of discerning *who* and *what* is the person. Nursing is the affirmation, support, and the celebration of the whole person at any single moment. Because nursing is envisioned as a continuing process, it is an on-going, knowledgeable practice. As such, the use of technologies in nursing form the perspective for caring and allows nurses to know all that can be known in the moment.

From this expression of nursing, caring is described as "the intentional and authentic presence of the nurse….[in which] the nurse endeavors to come to know the other fully as a caring person seeking to understand how that person might be supported, sustained, and strengthened in her or his living and growing in caring" (Boykin and Schoenhofer, 2001, p. 13). Caring is a substantive area of nursing requiring continuing study. As such, knowledge that is gained about the person, continually contributes to the body of extant knowledge that supports the professional practice of nursing that is theoretically framed and evidence based.

In appreciating the practice model of technological competency as caring, the following assumptions are offered:

- Persons are whole or complete in any moment (Boykin & Schoenhofer, 2001).
- Knowing persons is a process of nursing that allows the continuous understanding of persons as whole and complete from moment to moment.

118

- Nursing is a discipline and a professional practice.
- Technology is used to know persons as whole and complete at any particular moment.

Persons are Whole and Complete in Any Moment

One of the earlier definitions of the word "person" can be found in Hudson's 1988 publication in which the "emphasis on inclusive rather than sexist language has brought into prominence the use of the word 'person'" (p. 12). The origin of the word person is derived from the Greek word *prosopon*, which means the actor's mask of Greek tragedy. In Roman origin, *persona* is defined as the role played by the individual in social or legal relationships. According to Hudson, "An individual in isolation is contrary to an understanding of 'person'" (p.15). Thus, the use of the word "person" when used to describe technological competence clearly suggests the nurse is aware of the importance of seeing the person as more than parts of the self.

In this model, persons are viewed as human beings who are whole or complete in any moment. As such, there is no need to fix them or to make them whole again. Inherent in humans as unpredictable, dynamic, and living beings is the regard for self as a unique person. This appreciation is like the human concern for security and safety. In appreciating this quality of a person, human beings possess the prerogative and the choice whether or not to allow nurses to know her or him fully as a person. However, entering the world of another is a critical requisite to knowing that person, so establishing rapport, trust, confidence, commitment, and the compassion to know the other fully as a person is essential for the professional nurse and for the one who is nursed.

> The expectation as nurse is to use multiple ways of knowing in the fullness of possibilities, competently using technologies to know the other fully as a person.

Measures of Wholeness

As a model, technological competency as caring in nursing is a valuable practice. The future may require a different appreciation of who or what is a person, thus the completely human person is the ideal—the one fully alive with functional human organs. However, this complete human being may not totally exist in the future. For instance, what structural requirements will the post human possess? Even today, there are some human beings who have anatomic and/or physiologic components that are already electronic and/or mechanical. For example, many people have a mechanical cardiac valve, a self-injecting insulin pump, a cardiac pacemaker, or artificial limbs—all creating wholeness for the person—a quantifiable phenomenon.

Barnard (1996) emphasized the need for viewing human beings as persons even though they have technological parts such as metallic joints and replacements for bones because of disease or loss, pacemakers, hearing aides, facial lifts, augmented breasts, or penile implants. According to Prout (1996), in situations wherein technology comprises the human, "the human and the technology mutually constitute each other and thus cannot be understood as entities apart from each other"(p. 369). One is in the other, as opposed to the one (that is, the technological) existing exclusively as outside the human (Gadow, 1984).

Wholeness of Persons

Trust is imperative! The person must be able to trust that the nurse will not judge nor stereotype her or him as just another human being or experience. Instead, the nurse must be able to view the person as someone unique with hopes, dreams, and aspirations that are uniquely her or his own.

> There is one certainty about a person: A person is a human being.

It is the nurse's responsibility to know the person's hopes, dreams, and aspirations. In doing so, the nurse also sanctions the other (the nursed) to know her or him as person. The expectation as nurse is to use multiple ways of knowing the person by competently using technologies. The nurse's responsibility is significant in creating the conditions that support technological competency and care.

Conceptualizations of Persons as Whole

While there are many ways of interpreting the concept of person as whole, there is one certainty about a person: A person is a human being. Varying worldviews and paradigm shifts influence the interpretation and understanding of concepts. For example, there are many interpretations of nursing as professional practice. Interpretations are derivations of the concept from a dominant perspective. They are views that shape the popular understanding of the concept. As such, these interpretations often create a popularized conception of a human being. It is apparently clear that being a human being is being a person. What follows are some of the interpretations that delineate the exclusivity of disciplinary conceptions that influence healthcare practices.

Those of the bio-behavioral disciplines, including medicine, define "person as whole" as a composite of the parts. Such organismic or mechanical views of a person are derived from a positivist perspective that suggests an understanding that the parts create a comprehension of the whole. Such a view explains the nature of medical practice—the cure or fixing of human beings who have parts. As such, the objective of the practice is the summation of the parts. Each functional unit, for example the respiratory system, the musculo-skeletal system, and the neurological system, is identified and the malfunctioning part is repaired using a procedural recipe of diagnoses, treatment, and knowledge from various sciences such as anatomy, physiology, biochemistry, pharmacology, and so on.

Another view of "persons as whole" exists. It is the concept of wholeness from a view of mutuality that is purported to exist between human beings and the environment. This view of the person dictates human beings be viewed as unpredictable and complete moment to moment and not needing fixing or to be made whole again (Boykin & Schoenhofer, 2001). This view of human beings requires a distinction of nursing practice as integral to the appreciation of wellness, quality of life, or health from an individual's view, and the prospect of wellness of a community of persons.

Martha Rogers (1970) proposed what she called the "science of unitary human beings" as a way of understanding human beings. This interpretation described the physical nature of human beings as less likely to dictate the description of human beings as persons requiring nursing. This perspective underscores the fluidity of being a human being. It debunks the rigid description of human beings as entities made up of parts, whose completeness or wholeness is the only criterion that makes them human, and the only reason for a need of healthcare.

Technology in Nursing

Technology for most is understood as a means to an end, a tool, or an instrument (Heidegger, 1977). While the concept of technology is often interpreted as machine technology, in this book it is viewed as one of the many ways of understanding human behavior relative to healthcare.

> Cardiac monitors are technological instruments and the interpretation of the monitor data is a human activity.

Various definitions of technology exist, but one that fits nursing well is Heidegger's (1977) interpretation that technology is a means to an end, as well as a human activity. For example, cardiac monitors are technological instruments and the interpretation of the monitor data is a human activity. Information acquired through cardiac monitoring is used as a basis for the human activities of medical and nursing personnel who maintain a patient's well-being.

Using Bush's (1983) definition of technology as people, equipment, and procedures in established patterns of interactions for the purpose of accomplishing human goals, Sandelowski (1993) describes "technology dependency" as a reliance on equipment and techniques to manage the healthcare of patients. The effect of technology in nursing practice is also discussed by Cooper (1993) who describes critical care units as places where the challenge of using and interpreting machine technology is greatest. In these settings, machines provide life support to patients and are vital to patient care management.

Technological competency in nursing is the ability to use healthcare technologies to continually know and understand the patient as whole or complete in the moment. It is the expert use of available technologies in order to know and understand what is important to the person and what is needed to facilitate the person's ability to live out her or his hopes, dreams, and aspirations.

Caring in Nursing

Caring as a substantive component of nursing has directed much attention to its definition and the varying conceptualizations of its use in the practice of nursing. The pressure for professional nurses to achieve greater technological proficiency has fostered a re-thinking of the technology-caring dichotomy. Caring has gained prominence as a central component of nursing. The current emphasis on technologic competency for quality nursing practice and the dependence on machine technology have achieved a distinction that is significant to the practice of nursing. To fully care in this increasingly sophisticated world, nurses generally recognize that technologic proficiency is a desirable attribute and not a substitute for caring but an important variation of caring.

> To fully care in this increasingly sophisticated world, nurses generally recognize that technologic proficiency is a desirable attribute—not a substitute for caring but an important aspect of caring.

Caring in nursing has been described in a variety of ways (Leininger, 1988; Watson, 1985). Discussions of the issues of caring in nursing, (Jacono, 1993; Olson, 1993; Phillips, 1993; Swanson, 1993) attributes of caring (Roach, 1987), and ingredients of caring (Mayeroff, 1971) all illustrate the current significance of the concept of caring. Leininger (1988) claims that caring is the unifying feature of nursing and that caring is the common link that brings nurses together. In like manner, Watson (1990) emphasizes that caring is the moral ideal of nursing, while Roach (1992) considers caring to be a human mode of being.

The interactive nature of caring requires mutual commitment from the one giving care and the one being cared for. Phillips (1993) described caring in nursing as requiring the one giving care to respond to the needs of the other. Boykin and Schoenhofer (2001) describe caring as being intentionally and authentically present for another.

The competent use of machine technology as an integral part of caring has been advanced by several scholars of nursing including Cooper (1993), Jones and Alexander (1993), Ray (1987), and Sandelowski (1993). For some, competence with machines and equipment in technologically demanding environments is the ultimate expression of caring in nursing and technologic incompetence is tantamount to not caring.

Descriptions of a the Technology-Caring Dichotomy in Nursing

Nurse scholars and practitioners are constantly searching for useful ways to understand and improve the practice of nursing. Boykin's and Schoenhofer's (2001) general theory of Nursing as Caring grounds the model of technological competency as caring in nursing. They posit that nursing occurs within nursing situations—shared and lived experiences between the nurse and the person being nursed. Within this nursing situation, the nurse hears, expresses, and addresses the calls for nursing expressed by the nursed who seeks to be known and affirmed as a caring person. The nurse enters the world of the other with the intention of knowing the other as a caring person. The nurse's responses are specific forms of caring created for each unique situation. In this process of nursing, each person grows in competency, including technological competency, in order to express herself or himself as a caring person.

Cooper (1993) states that machines and equipment are designed to be invulnerable, objective, and predictable, in contrast to the human characteristics of vulnerability, subjectivity, and unpredictability, thereby challenging professional nurses to be technologically competent while simultaneously recognizing human vulnerability when responding authentically and intentionally to calls for nursing. Authenticity and intentionality are demonstrated when a nurse appropriately accepts the patient's care as requiring high levels of technical expertise. In doing so, the nurse focuses her or his activities toward knowing the person fully as a caring person.

> Machines and equipment are designed to be invulnerable, objective, and predictable. These features stand in contrast to the human characteristics of vulnerability, subjectivity, and unpredictability.

Nursing technologies and caring are the core structures. Technological competency is exemplified by nursing assistants who are ordered to use tools and other instruments in order to determine the physiological condition of the patient. A professional nurse who is technologically competent but who has little other knowledge of the patient is a caregiver who is not truly caring. Understanding technological competency as caring in nursing is a way to know a patient more fully as a person and is an expression of the harmonious existence between technology and caring in nursing.

Proficiency in technological use without it being grounded in a nursing perspective is simply technological competency. As people who are seriously involved in giving care know, there are various ways of expressing caring, such as a touch, a reassuring comment, or the prompt response to a request. However, professional nurses must continue to find meaning in their technological caring by knowing the other fully as a whole person. Through the harmonious coexistence of machine technology and caring in nursing, the practice of nursing is transformed anew. Professionals and patients alike can only be grateful for the vast advances in medical and machine technology. However, their inclusion must not compromise nurses' care. As professional nurses become more and more technically adept,

References

Barnard, A., & Sandelowski, M. (2001). Technology and humane nursing care: (Ir)reconcilable or invented difference? *Journal of Advanced Nursing, 34*(4), 367-375.

Boykin, A., & Schoenhofer, S. (2001). *Nursing as caring: A model for transforming practice*. New York: Jones & Bartlett, National League for Nursing Press.

Burfitt, S., Greiner, D., Miers, L., Kinney, M., & Branyon, M. (1993). Professional nurse caring as perceived by critically ill patients: A phenomenologic study. *American Journal of Critical Care, 2*(6), 489-499.

Carper, B. (1977). Fundamental patterns of knowing in nursing. *Advances in Nursing Science, 1*(1), 13-24.

Cooper, M. (1993). The intersection of technology and care in the ICU. *Advances in Nursing Science, 15*(3), 23-32.

Gadow, S. (1984). Touch and technology: Two paradigms of patient care. *Journal of Religion and Health, 23*(63), 150-169.

Heidegger, M. (1977). *The question concerning technology and other essays.* New York: Harper & Row.

Hudson, R. (1988). Whole or parts–a theological perspective on "person." *The Australian Journal of Advanced Nursing, 6*(1), 12-20.

Jones, C., & Alexander, J. (1993). The technology of caring: A synthesis of technology and caring for nursing administration. *Nursing Administration Quarterly, 17*(2), 11-20.

Leininger, M. (1988). Leininger's theory of nursing: Cultural care diversity and universality. *Nursing Science Quarterly, 1*, 152-160.

Locsin, R. (1995). Machine technologies and caring in nursing. *Image: Journal of Nursing Scholarship, 27*(3), 201-203.

Locsin, R. (1998). Technologic competence as expression of caring in critical care settings. *Holistic Nursing Practice, 12*(4), 50-56.

Lynaugh, J., & Fagin, C. (1988). Nursing outcomes of age. *Image: Journal of Nursing Scholarship, 20*(4), 184-190.

Mayeroff, M. (1971). *On caring.* New York: Harper & Row.

Olson, T. (1993). Laying claim to caring: Nursing and the language of training, 1915-1937. *Nursing Outlook, 41*(2), 68-72.

Phillips, P. (1993). A deconstruction of caring. *Journal of Advanced Nursing, 18,* 1554-1558.

Porter, S. (1992). The poverty of professionalization: A critical analysis of strategies for the occupational advancement of nursing. *Journal of Advanced Nursing, 17,* 723-728.

Prout A. (1996) Actor-network theory, technology and medical sociology: an illustrative analysis of the metered dose inhaler. *Sociology of Health & Illness 18,* 198–219.

Ray, M. (1987). Technological caring: A new model in critical care. *Dimensions in Critical Care, 6*(3), 166-73.

Roach, S. (1987). *The human act of caring.* Ottawa, Canada: Canadian Hospital Association.

Rogers, M. (1970). Introduction to theoretical bases of nursing. Philadelphia: F.A. Davis.

Sandelowski, M. (1993). Toward a theory of technology dependency. *Nursing Outlook, 41*(1), 36-42.

Swanson, K. (1993). Nursing as informed caring for the well-being of others. *Image: Journal of Nursing Scholarship, 25*(4), 352-357.

Watson, J. (1985). *Nursing: The philosophy and science of caring.* Boulder, CO: Colorado Associated University Press.

8

CHAPTER

Knowing Persons as a Framework for Nursing Practice

By Rozzano C. Locsin

Nursing practice is guided by many processes. As such, these various processes are derived from theories of nursing. One of these processes is "knowing about the patient through technological competency." This process involves a continuous collection of data in order to understand the person as whole and complete in the moment through the competent use of technologies of nursing. For what is more important than knowing the other as a unique person? In knowing the person, the nurse uses all possible means she or he has, allowing for the collection, analysis, and interpretation of all of the person's calls for nursing, as well as for the origination and implementation of responses to these calls for nursing. Altogether, these activities permit the nurse to continuously know the person fully as whole and as a complete human being. Such a dynamic process prevents the objectification of human beings who assume roles in healthcare.

Nursing is a dynamic unfolding of situations based on knowledgeable practices. It is characterized by listening, knowing, being with, enabling, and maintaining belief (Swanson, 1991). The following activities exemplify the process.

- Knowing and appreciating the uniqueness of persons.
- Designing participation in caring.
- Implementation and evaluation. (A simultaneous exercise of conjoining relationships crucial to knowing persons through using nursing technologies.)
- Verifying knowledge of the person through continuous data collection.

In this model of nursing practice, knowing is the prime process. "Knowing [in] nursing means knowing in the realms of personal, ethical, empirical and aesthetic—all at once" (Boykin & Schoenhofer, 2001, p. 6). This continuous, circular process demonstrates the ever-changing, dynamic, cyclical nature of knowing in nursing. Knowledge about the patient that is derived from assessment, intervention, evaluation, and further assessment informs the nurse that in knowing the patient, one comes to understand more about him or her, and that there are more aspects that the nurse does not know about the patient. This process of knowing is supported by the belief that persons are unpredictable, that they simultaneously conceal and reveal themselves as persons from moment to moment; the nurse can only know the patient fully in a situated moment in time. This knowing occurs only when the patient allows the nurse to enter her or his world. At this time, the nurse and patient become vulnerable to further continuous knowing.

Vulnerability allows participation so much so that the nurse and nursed continue knowing each other in the moment. In such situations, Daniel (1998) explains "nurse's work to ameliorate vulnerability" (p. 191). This vulnerability in caring situations enables both the nurse and the patient to share in the humanness of being vulnerable. As Daniel declares, "Vulnerable individuals seek nursing care, and nurses seek those who are vulnerable" (p. 192). Allowing the nurse to enter the world of the patient is the mutual engagement of "power with" rather than having "power over" through a created hierarchy (Daniels 1998). The nurse does not know more about the patient than she or he knows about herself or himself.

Nonetheless, there is the possibility that the nurse will need to predict and prescribe for the patient. When this occurs, the nurse is likely to view the patient more as an object than as a person. Such situations can occur only when the nurse has presumed to have known the patient. While it can be presumed, with the process of knowing persons as whole, opportunities to continuously know the other become limitless. There is also a much greater likelihood that having already known the patient, the nurse will predict and prescribe activities for the patient, with objectification ultimately occurring. However, when knowing is viewed as a continuous process and "power with" is employed, this possibility can be limited.

> Allowing the nurse to enter the world of the patient is the mutual engagement of "power with" rather than having "power over" through a created hierarchy.

Knowing Persons as a Process of Nursing Care

It is interesting to note that there are 10 verb definitions of the word "know" listed in the *Reader's Digest Illustrated Encyclopedic Dictionary* (1987, p. 932). Nine appropriately fit the intent and meaning of the purpose and process of technological competency as caring in nursing. These descriptions are:

1. To perceive directly with the senses or mind.
2. To be certain of; regard or accept as true beyond doubt.
3. To be capable of; have the skill to.
4. To have thorough or practical understanding of; as through experience of.
5. To be subjected to or limited by.
6. To recognize the character or quality of.
7. To be able to distinguish; recognize.
8. To be acquainted or familiar with.
9. To see, hear, or experience.

While the action verb "know" sustains the notion that nursing is concerned with activity and that the one who acts is knowledgeable in the sense of understanding the rationale behind an activity, another key concept that alludes to the focus of an action from a cognitive perspective that requires description is the word "knowing." Surprisingly, the *Reader's Digest Illustrated Encyclopedic Dictionary* (1987) attributes its definition as an adjective. Posited are the four adjectival descriptions:

- Possessing knowledge, intelligence, or understanding.
- Suggestive of secret or private information.
- Having or showing clever awareness and resourcefulness.
- Planned; deliberate.

Yet, "knowing" as a gerund form of the verb "to know" perfectly describes the ways that it provides the framework of knowing persons as a process in nursing. This use of the word in practice clearly demonstrates the circuitous process of knowing persons within the practice of nursing.

While it is expected that nurses practice nursing from a theoretical perspective rather than from tradition or blind obedience to instructions and directions, the processes of nursing that are derived from extant theories of nursing continue to dictate, often prescribing how a nurse should function following that particular theory. Contrary to this popular belief is the "knowing persons" model of practice, where the use of technologies of nursing provide the nurse with an appreciation of the expertise needed, along with the realization that although technologies allow nurses to know much about the patient the actual knowledge of the patient is limited to that which she or he permits the nurse to know. It is true that technologies detect the anatomical, physiological, chemical, and biological conditions of the patient. This is "what is the person." However, the nurse can also know "who is the person?" Answers to this question allow the nurse to understand the person as whole human being.

Nonetheless, the information derived from knowing the person is only relevant for the moment, for that person's state can change moment to moment, which is a realization of the dynamic, living, unpredictable human being. Importantly, knowing the who or what of patients helps to make concrete the fact that people are more than simply a physiochemical and anatomical being. Knowing persons allows the nurse to know who the person is, the nurses' intention to care (Locsin & Purnell, 1997), the continuing appreciation of the ever-changing person—never static, but rather dynamic.

> The idea that knowing persons guides nursing practice is novel in the sense that there is no prescription or direction that is the ideal; rather there is the wholesome appreciation of a practice that allows the use of multiple ways of knowing.

From such a view, one could conclude that the process of knowing is only possible when technologies are used. This is not necessarily true. This perception is supported by the idea that nursing is technology when technology is appreciated as anything that creates efficiency, be it an instrument, a machine, or the activity of nurses. Sandelowski (1999) has argued about the metaphorical depiction of nursing as technology or with technology as nursing, and the semiotic relationship of these concepts. Regardless, the idea of knowing persons as a guide for nursing practice is novel in the sense that there is no prescription or direction that is the ideal; rather, there is the wholesome appreciation of an informed practice that allows the use of multiple ways of knowing as described by Phenix (1964) and expanded by Carper (1978). These ways of knowing involve the empirical, ethical, personal, and aesthetic. Guiding this process are the four fundamental patterns of knowing identified by Carper (1978): empirics, aesthetics, ethics, and personal. These patterns can be appreciated as:

- The use of aesthetic expressions.
- The use of documentation.
- The use of communication.
- The perpetuation of the appreciation of nurses.

There is no letting up, for advancing technology currently encompasses the bulk of functional activities nurses are expected to perform when the practice is in clinical settings

Popular among these patterns of knowing are storytelling, poetry recitation, visual expressions (as in drawings, illustrations, and paintings), and aural renditions (such as vocal and instrumental music). Using aesthetic expressions allows the nurse and the patient to relive the occasion. Reflecting on these experiences using the fundamental patterns of knowing, enhances learning, motivates the furtherance of knowledgeable practice, and increases the valuing of nursing as a professional practice grounded in a legitimate theoretical perspective of nursing.

The use of technologies in nursing is consequent to the contemporary demands for nursing actions that require proficiency with advancing technologies. There is no letting up, for advancing technology currently encompasses the bulk of functional activities nurses are expected to perform when the practice is in clinical settings. Clinical nursing is firmly rooted in the clinical health model (Smith, 1983) where the organismic and mechanistic views of human beings convincingly dictate the practice of nursing. Nevertheless, the process of knowing persons will prevail, for the model provides the nurse with the stimulation, motivation, and the potential autonomy to critically decide modes of action that allow for appreciations of the whole patient.

The model demands continuous knowing. Continuing to know persons deters objectification, a process that ultimately regards human beings as objects of care rather than as participants in care. Participating in her or his care frees the patient from having imposed care that she or he may not want or need. This relationship signifies responsiveness (Hudson, 1988). Continuous knowing results from the contention that findings or information appreciated through consequent knowing further informs the desire to know "who is" and "what is" the person. Doing so inhibits substantiation. It overpowers the motivation to prescribe and direct the patient's life; instead it affirms, supports, and celebrates her or his hopes, dreams, and aspirations as a human being.

Calls and Responses for Nursing

Calls for nursing are ways the person expresses hopes, dreams, and aspirations. Calls for nursing are the ways people seek affirmation, support, and celebration as a human being. The nurse appreciates the uniqueness of each person. In doing so, the nurse sustains and enhances the wholeness of that person and facilitates her or his completeness by acting for or with the person.

The nurse relies on the patient to present the call for nursing. These calls are specific mechanisms used by the patient that allow the nurse to respond with authentic intentions to know the person fully in the moment. Calls for nursing may be expressed in many ways—oftentimes as hopes and dreams—such as hoping to be with friends while recuperating in the hospital, expressing a desire to play the piano when her or his fingers are healed and able to function effectively, or simply the ultimate desire to go home and die peacefully. As uniquely as these calls for nursing are expressed, the nurse knows the person continuously moment to moment. The created nursing responses may be communicated as patterns of relating information, such as those derived from machines like the EKG monitor—in order to know the physiological status of the person in the moment—or the administration of life-saving medications, or a transfer plan, or a referral for services to other healthcare professionals. The nursing actions direct, focus, attain, sustain, and maintain for the patient. In doing so, hearing calls for nursing is continuous, momentary, and complete.

There is a great demand for a practice of nursing that is based on the authentic desire to know human beings as persons rather than as objects of care. Through authentic intentions and desires, the nurse is challenged to use every creative, imaginative, and innovative way possible to appreciate and celebrate the person's intentions to live fully and grow as a human being. Only with expertise in technologies is the expression of technological competence realized.

Ways of Knowing Through a Nursing Lens

Nursing based on a framework of nursing as caring (Boykin & Schoenhofer, 2001) provides the grounding for technological competency as caring by directing the focus of nursing to knowing persons as whole in the moment. Every human being responds uniquely to personal conditions in the moment. The nurse understands that the process of nursing occurs without preconceived views to categorize a person as needing to be fixed. By allowing the human being to unfold as a person with hopes, dreams, and aspirations to live fully as a human being, nursing is perpetuated as a caring process that transpires between the person and nurse in the moment.

Nurses use technologies to address the calls for nursing so they can fully know the patient. The empirical, personal, ethical, and aesthetic ways of knowing which are fundamental to understanding persons as whole increase the likelihood of reaching that goal. As unpredictable and dynamic, human beings are ever-changing. This characteristic challenges the nurse to know persons continuously as whole in the moment, discouraging and ceasing the traditional idea of possibly knowing persons completely in order to prescribe and predict their expressions of wholeness and perhaps intervene to make them whole again.

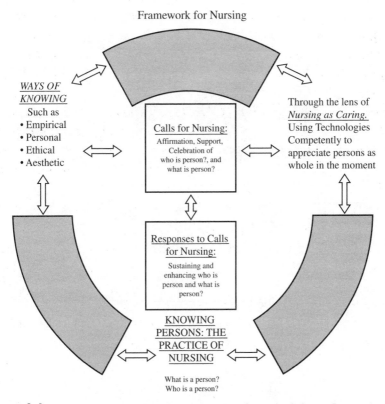

Figure 8.1. *Nursing is grounded in the appreciation of person wholeness. Its practice is founded in the process of knowing persons as whole and complete in the moment. Patterns of knowing (Carper, 1978) through the lens of Nursing as Caring (Boykin and Schoenhofer, 2001) using technologies competently in order to appreciate persons as whole and complete in the moment, simultaneously and laternately influence appreciating Calls for Nursing (affirming, supporting, celebrating person wholeness in the moment), and responding to these Calls to sustain and enhance person wholeness. Knowing persons is the practice of nursing.*

Errata sheet for page 138 of Technological Competency as Caring in Nursing: A Model for Practice.

TECHNOLOGICAL COMPETENCY AS CARING

References

Boykin, A., & Schoenhofer, S. (2001). *Nursing as caring: A model for transforming practice*. New York: Jones & Bartlett, National League for Nursing Press.

Carper, B. (1978). Fundamental patterns of knowing in nursing. *Advances in Nursing Science, 1*, 13-24.

Daniels, L. (1998). Vulnerability as a key to authenticity. *Image: Journal of Nursing Scholarship, 30*(2), 191-192.

Hudson, R. (1988). Whole or parts–a theological perspective on "person." *The Australian Journal of Advanced Nursing, 6*(1), 12-20

Phenix, P. (1964). *Realms of meaning*. New York: McGraw-Hill.

Reader's Digest Illustrated Encyclopedic Dictionary. (1987). Pleasantville, New York: The Reader's Digest Association, Inc.

Roach, S. (1987). *The human act of caring*. Ottawa, Canada: Canadian Hospital Association.

Reed, J., & Ground, I. (1997). *Philosophy for nursing*. London: Arnold Press.

Sandelowski, M. (1999). Troubling distinctions: A semiotics of the nursing/technology relationship. *Nursing Inquiry, 6*, 198-207.

Smith, J. (1983). *The idea of health*. New York: Teachers College Press.

Swanson, K. (1993). Nursing as informed caring for the well-being of others. *Image: Journal of Nursing Scholarship, 25*(4), 352-357.

ublished by Sigma Theta Tau International ISBN: 1-930538-12-X

3

PART

Practical Approaches to the Model in Care Situations

9

CHAPTER

Techno Sapiens and Post Humans: Nursing, Caring, and Technology

By Rozzano C. Locsin and
Aric S. Campling

The functional human being with the physical and functional features and characteristics of a true human being is easily distinguished and defined. What, then, if the functional human being possesses mechanical or electronic parts that perpetuate human functioning? Is this human being a person? Advancing technologies increasingly provide more human-like mechanical or electronic parts that enhance the characteristics and features of a human being. Today more than ever before, nursing and its usual practice is acutely analyzed, doubted, and more readily pushed toward a functional practice relegated as routine actions of simple, technological savvy. The value of technological expertise or competencies with technologies affecting human function are desired; however, popular consequences of economics and satisfaction are derived more efficiently when a desired practice provides the consequent results of financial gain and satisfaction.

Nevertheless, the transcendence of nursing as a practice of knowing persons who are whole and complete in the moment and who require intentional, authentic, and integral care is crucial to living life more fully as persons. The appreciation of persons with aspects that declare what we call human life is integral to nursing practice. One of these integral aspects is human intelligence.

Artificial Intelligence

In the 1966 science fiction novel *The Moon is a Harsh Mistress*, Robert Heinlein (1997) tells the life story of a computer who gains self-awareness. Mycroft, as the computer is named, is able to convince all who see, hear, and interact with his public persona that he is, despite being made of metal and circuits, a person. One character has this to say about Mycroft's sense of self: "Somewhere along the evolutionary chain from macromolecule to human brain, self-awareness crept in. Psychologists say it happens automatically when a brain acquires certain very high numbers of associational paths. Can't see it matters whether paths are protein or platinum" (p. 12).

Only sixteen years earlier, Alan Turing (1950) had proposed the question, "can machines think?" (p. 433). Turing defends a vision for the future of machine intelligence. He states that an entity that could successfully fool an impartial interrogator into believing, as often as not, that it is human, can be considered an intelligent, thinking machine. Though Turing made no strong argument that computers or machines could be made to think intelligently, he did generate guidelines for building learning machines that might be taught, over time, to interact with people at the level of a human adult (Turing, 1950, Moravec, 1999).

Altman (1997) expanded upon Turing's theory of intelligence by outlining four general characteristics of an intelligent act. The first of these characteristics is *flexibility*. Flexibility includes the ability to self-correct and devise novel solutions to a problem. The second characteristic is *multiplexity*, an activity that features acts exhibiting multiple solutions to the same problem. *Generalization* allows an encompassing solution to be applied to a new and different situation, while *insight* describes the sudden change in the trial-and-error learning curve followed by an absence of regression to trial-and-error attempts to determine an appropriate action in a given situation.

> Is the fact that Kismet thrives on social interaction, is learning how to behave in a human manner, enough to call Kismet a person?

Cynthia Brazeal, a postdoctoral associate at the artificial intelligence lab at Massachusetts Institute of Technology (MIT) describes the Kismet project. Kismet is a sociable machine, a robotic head that interacts with people in a human-like way through facial expressions, head and eye positions, and tones of voice. Kismet does not yet know English, but he "speaks" in a gibberish language (Brooks, 2002). The goal is to create a machine that learns through social interaction, the way humans learn. Kismet has been able to engage people in conversation for hours at a time, while others cannot stay with it for more than a few minutes (Brooks, 2002). Is the fact that Kismet thrives on social interaction, is learning how to behave in a human manner, enough to call Kismet a person? Alternatively, is Kismet simply a fantastic, unique machine? Or both?

The Human, the Person

Pollock (1989) argues that the concept of person can include various, differing physiologies. By extension, "something is a person if its ... interactions appropriately mimic human rational architecture" (p. 111). While this mimicry ascribes human-like features as a requisite to being human, Blackmore (1999) decidedly addressed the concept of "meme," the "element of a culture that may be considered to be passed on by non-genetic means, especially imitation" (Old English Dictionary) as characteristic of the human mind. Dawkins (1999) alludes to this memetic as the familiarity of human behavior such as the unconscious imitation of other human beings, especially parental roles or those we admire. The resulting entity connected to the world in an appropriate manner, therefore, may be defined as a person according to this definition. The form this entity takes would not matter and could very well be a complete computer model of human rational thought; physiology is immaterial (Pollock, 1989, Turing, 1950). Therefore, what defines a person? Is it the physicality, intelligence, emotion, or something greater? Does it matter that humans or machines have physicality at all, or is it as Turing or Pollock may argue—that physicality only distracts us from the reality of the intelligence behind the physical façade (Turing, 1950, Pollock, 1989)?

> "Technological advancement presents new challenges to nursing practice and theory. While the concept of the fully sentient computer we envision is not yet a reality, we are quickly advancing toward a point where humans are becoming more mechanical."

Technology, Nursing, and Caring

Brazeal (2001) declares that people are often afraid that technology is making human beings less human. This statement rings particularly true as a major concern in nursing, particularly of our understanding of the persons being nursed. Technology is the enhancement of anything in nature which then becomes more efficient. This idea is critical to the practice of nursing. Sandelowski (2000) clearly addresses this description of technology and proposes a rethinking of the appreciation of nursing as technology and of technology as nursing.

Technological advancement presents new challenges to nursing practice and theory. While the concept of the fully sentient computer we envision is not yet a reality, we are quickly advancing toward a point where humans are becoming more mechanical. The increasing popularity of replacement and mechanical parts, and the increasing use of advanced life support measures, demand that nurses re-visit the meaning of person as the focus of nursing practice.

The person as whole is the focus of nursing (Boykin & Schoenhofer, 2001). Persons as we understand them now are human beings, whose composition, characteristics, and descriptions are structured from views of wholeness. These views of wholeness are derived from conceptualizations within paradigms grounding theories of nursing. Two distinct descriptions of wholeness are presented by Parse (1993). From the perspective of the totality paradigm, human beings are described as whole and as the summation of various composing parts. It is possible to know the person through the part that is affected and studied. The simultaneity paradigm addresses the conception of wholeness as the mutuality, regardless of composition of features and physical parts, and the affirmation and celebration of persons as more than and different from the sum of their parts.

Appreciating human beings from the totality paradigm is popular and practical in a traditional practice of nursing, rather than the appreciation of nursing as a substantive knowledge grounding its practice. The typical understanding of persons as a composite of parts is slowly becoming outmoded for nursing. Technology has enabled the reshaping and replacement of body parts, as well as the prolongation of life—even after a medically diagnosed brain death. Technological advances challenge the concept of a whole person by drawing focus to the technological parts and extensions, which may disrupt the understanding of person-as-whole.

Essentially, advances in artificial intelligence and robot technology may soon pose credible threats to a traditional concept of the *human being* as person.

Transhumanity and the Post Human

The primary focus of nursing is knowing the human being as a person. In describing "person," a variety of delineations may exist. The basic criterion of many nursing theories describes persons as human beings who are whole and complete (Boykin & Schoenhofer, 2001). Contemporary appreciation of humans with mechanical and replacement parts, and futuristic descriptions of post human beings such as techno-sapiens, neomorts, and cyborgs are vivid examples of the distinctive characteristics that challenge the concept of person. The humanness characteristic, then, becomes the critical criterion for furthering the understanding of persons as the focus of nursing. Who, or what, is person? How do nurses come to know the person? Does knowing in nursing involve affirming and celebrating persons as whole? On the other hand, is it simply that nursing is the knowing of parts and the completion of persons?

> **"Technology has enabled the reshaping and replacement of body parts, as well as the prolongation of life—even after a medically diagnosed brain death."**

Transhumanism

Colin Tudge (1996) stated that, "There is no *a priori* reason why a human being should not combine the qualities ... of Einstein, Shakespeare, Mozart, Darwin, a nuthatch, and a pocket calculator. Indeed, there is no *a priori* reason why such a paragon should not be considered ordinary" (para. 29). The essence of transhumanity is that humans can, and should, continue to develop in all possible directions. The bodies and minds that evolution has provided for humanity are wonderful, but far from perfect. They can be improved in many ways, and this can be done in a rational manner using science and technology (Tudge, 1996). In the end, we will no longer be human beings any more; instead, we will be post human beings.

The Post Human Being

For the post human, the main consideration is embodiment. Should the body be seen as evolutionary baggage that we are able to toss out as we vault into the brave new post-human world? Is this necessarily a bad thing? Even now, people are willing (and oftentimes required) to trade in their old parts for newer, better replacements, or have augmentations to their existing parts made so they will perform better. Moravec (1999) envisions a future in which people can routinely perfect their existing biology through mechanical and biological means—but that these enhanced beings would be required to relinquish their right to call themselves human. However, Hayles (2000) has cautioned that it is critical that we find ways to describe and build the post human without supposing corporeal appearance as the indispensable basis for recognizing human existence. Many variations of the post human appearance—having a head possessing capacities for vision, respiration, hearing, and vocalization structures—oftentimes comprise the creative rendering of the post human. Perhaps it is the human need to express the idea of continuing or furthering the human species, which likely sets the stage for visualizing transhumans or the post human.

Techno-Sapiens, Neomorts, and Cyborgs

Techno sapien, a fusion of human and machine, is one embodiment of the post human being. Calonius (1996) states that the evolutionary tracks of humankind and technology are beginning to overlap. In the new relationship, technology is expanding the capability of the human beyond the limits imposed by flesh and blood alone (Calonius, 1996). The term techno sapiens conjures a race of flesh-and-technology beings who are physically superior and possess unnatural perceptual powers (Calonius, 1996).

The Cyborg

In 1960, Manfred Clynes and Nathan Kline, writing a report for NASA about the future of space travel, envisioned a future in which human beings no longer adapted environments to suit human capability for space travel, but instead adapted humans to the environment of space. They stated that the challenges of space flight invited humans to take an active part in our evolution (Clynes & Kline, 1960). Using advances in technology and the chemical, biological, and electronic sciences, human beings could be successfully altered to an extent such that improvements and adaptations could create a self-regulating combination of man-machine systems (Clynes & Kline, 1960). These systems would enable a body to survive the rigors of extended space travel and exploration. However, to free the human from the requirement of checking these additional systems to ensure life, the system must be self-regulating and automatic and therefore free the human to explore, create, think, and feel. Clynes and Kline (1960) propose the term cyborg to describe this "exogenously extended organizational complex, functioning as an integrated homeostatic system unconsciously" (p. 27). In other words, a combination of cybernetics— the comparative study of complex electronics and automatic nervous system controls (Principa Cybernetica, n.d.)— and organism. A cyborg.

> Perhaps it is the human need to express the idea of continuing or furthering the human species, which likely sets the stage for visualizing transhumans or the post human.

Since then, numerous others have studied the phenomenon of the cyborg, including Donna Haraway. Her Cyborg Manifesto (1991) defines cyborgs as creatures simultaneously animal and machine. However, she extends this to specify that cyborgs are certain kinds of machines and certain kinds of organisms (Haraway, 1991). She agrees that cyborgs have largely become a creature of fiction, but she argues that they are also a social reality (1991). Specifically, she identifies modern medicine as a source of cyborg entities, but then proceeds to argue that by the late 20th century everyone is already a chimera—a hybrid combination of human and machine (Haraway, 1991).

Not every technology-infused human being is a cyborg (though many may argue to the contrary). A person with a pacemaker might be a cyborg. However, to ensure effective functioning of a pacemaker, a technician must routinely monitor and adjust the instrument. A full, unconscious feedback mechanism between the pacemaker and the patient does not exist.

A person with an implanted osmotic pump might be considered a cyborg. The pump can be configured to detect certain physiological, bio-chemical markers within the body and dispense proper pharmaceuticals or bioactive elements directly to the appropriate organs or systems at appro-priate levels to maintain proper systemic homeostasis (Clynes & Kline, 1960). These functions occur without any direct, constant vigilance on behalf of the person. Such technology already exists in the form of an insulin pump for humans.

> "Not every technology-infused human being is a cyborg ... A person with a pacemaker might be a cyborg. However, to ensure effective functioning of a pacemak-er, a technician must routinely monitor and adjust the instrument. A full, unconscious feedback mechanism between the pacemaker and the patient does not exist."

Neomorts: The New Cadaver

In a cyborg system, the machines and systems that make up the extended complex function to sustain life do so under conditions that normal human bodies could not withstand. However, modern medical advances have allowed doctors and nurses to keep people alive by connecting them to machines that breathe for them, pump their hearts, and hydrate their cells.

Technology allows us to keep bodies physiologically alive even long after their brains have stopped all function. In 1974, William Gaylin detailed the potential to keep human bodies in such a state, capable of physiological regeneration, thus making them recyclable resources. Gaylin proposes a term for these new cadavers, whose visceral functions are kept intact and sustained, and whose vital functions are maintained—neomort. The neomort is a warm, respiring, evacuating, pulsating body that requires nutritional support, nursing support, and grooming support for a number of years (Gaylin, 1974). To the untrained eye, a neomort would be indistinguishable from a comatose patient. Gaylin further proposed the construction of hospital wards or units into what he called bioemporiums, where neomorts could be maintained and attended. These neomorts would then provide a steady supply of renewable, biological resources: blood, bone marrow, cartilage, and skin could be harvested; hormones, antitoxins, and antibodies could be manufactured in them (Gaylin, 1974). They could be used for studying medical assessments, except for neurological functioning, since neomorts, by definition, have no functioning central nervous system (Gaylin, 1974).

What are Persons?

Is this postmodern vision of humanity also a person? This brings us back to our fundamental question: What are human beings as persons?

Ultimately, however, the proverbial questions that nurses need to continuously ask should be, "who are the persons that nurses will nurse in the future? What should the nurse know or study when the focus of nursing are these kinds of persons with these kinds of parts—the post human beings? Attempting to guide answers to the aforementioned questions is the understanding that the focus of nursing practice is knowing persons; it is the practice of nursing. When persons such as previously described live life in their humanness, nursing practice exists as knowing who and what these persons are. Regardless, the notion of all persons as whole and complete in the moment is assumed in the general theory of Nursing as Caring (Boykin and Schoenhofer, 2001) meaningfully guides the practice of nursing as knowing persons as whole and complete in the moment.

Nursing as Caring

The assumption that nursing is both a discipline and a practice profession is assumed to guide the understanding of caring as a substantive knowledge (Boykin & Schoenhofer, 2001). The focus of nursing is nurturing the wholeness of persons through caring (Florida Atlantic University Philosophy Statement, 2002). All nursing takes place in moments of time, described as nursing situations. These situations are shared, lived experiences in which the caring between the nurse and the nursed enhances personhood which is expressed as living in caring and growing in caring (Boykin & Schoenhofer, 2001). While the situations of nursing occasions continue, the fact remains that various descriptions of nursing exist. These include definitions of nursing from a practice perspective such as Wiedenbach's nursing as a helping art (Wiedenbach, 1984); Roy's facilitating adaptation from varying internal and external stimuli (Roy & Corliss, 1993) and Rogers' knowing participation in change. Together, these practice perspectives declare that nursing practice, as a truly integral factor to nursing and health requires clarification of essential theoretical perspectives to support the legitimacy and critical nature of its practice.

Caring in Nursing

Caring is not unique to nursing, but it is unique in nursing (Roach, 2002, Boykin & Schoenhofer, 2001). Caring has been defined as the human mode of being (Roach, 2002). Roach's statement underscores the common understanding, experience, and practice of caring. Importantly, it addresses the uniqueness of caring that transpires in nursing. As a mode of being, caring dictates knowledgeable practice. With the intention to nurse, appreciating the value of being human acknowledges the person as whole and complete (Roach, 2002,

> The advent of technological marvels in sustaining human lives, viewed from the ideals of persons as whole and the many ways nursing practice is grounded in caring perspectives, underscores nursing as a caring discipline.

Boykin & Schoenhofer, 2001). Like Roach's appreciation of human beings as persons, caring is appreciating the "being of persons" in ways dictated by the nurse and the person being nursed.

Extending the value of caring, like Roach, Leininger (1992) declares that the fundamental nature of nursing is caring. Caring is a practice, a way of being with another person (Mayeroff, 1971). In this caring dynamic, both the person caring and the person being cared for grow, over time, as persons (Mayeroff, 1971). Human caring can only be effectively practiced interpersonally (Watson, 1999). Through the process of caring, the humanity of one is reflected in the humanity of the other (Watson, 1999). The ontology of the discipline of nursing is caring in the human health experience, as Newman, Sime, and Corcoran-Perry (1991) emphasize. It is in caring that we come to know and understand nursing (Boykin & Schoenhofer, 2001).

> As we move closer toward the post human, caring nursing theories must be flexible enough to accommodate new understandings of persons.

In like perspective, Boykin and Schoenhofer (2001), underscore the unity of caring as a substantive area for knowledge development in nursing. The phenomenon of interest in nursing is the "caring between" the nurse and the one nursed (Boykin & Schoenhofer, 2001). The appreciation of persons as complete moment to moment, and the understanding of nursing as transpiring between the nurses and nursed, declares the valuing of nursing practice as critical to healthcare.

Summary

The advent of technological marvels in sustaining human lives, viewed from the ideals of persons as whole and the many ways nursing practice is grounded in caring perspectives, underscores nursing as a caring discipline. Nursing theories variously temporize on the view of human beings as whole and complete in the moment, of nursing transpiring between the nurse and the one nursed, and the appreciation of health as quality of life. The appreciation of these concepts altogether dictate our understanding of how nursing is understood, how it is practiced, and how nursing is integral to healthcare.

Nursing is caring in the human health experience (Newman, 1997). The focus of nursing is the person. Through the lens of nursing as caring nursing, all persons are understood as caring by the virtue of their human-ness (Boykin & Schoenhofer, 2001). Persons are whole in the moment (of the nursing situation) in which nursing transpires. Health is quality of life as understood by the persons being cared for. Nursing is the practice of continually knowing persons as whole.

Technological advances, especially in modern medical and nursing practice, continue to challenge our definitions of personhood. As we move closer toward the post human, caring nursing theories must be flexible enough to accommodate new understandings of persons. Traditionally, the central focus of nursing care has dealt with the human being as this person. However, as modern and future advances in technology push toward our technological evolution, we will see cyborgs, neomorts, and other techno-sapiens as recipients of caring. What will nursing be, then?

References

Altman, I. (1997). *The concept of intelligence: A philosophical analysis*. New York: University Press of America.

Bell, J. (2002). Technotopia and the death of nature. *Earth Island Journal, 17*(2), 36-39.

Boykin, A., & Schoenhofer, S.O. (2001). *Nursing as caring: A model for transforming practice*. New York: Jones & Bartlett, National League for Nursing Press.

Brooks, R.A. (2002). *Flesh and machines: How robots will change us*. New York: Pantheon.

Calonius, E. (1996, July 8). Techno sapiens: The convergence of humans and technology. *Fortune, 134*, 73-76.

Clynes, M.E., & Kline, N.S. (1960). Cyborgs and space. *Astronautics*, 26-27, 74-76.

Gaylin, W. (1974). Harvesting the dead. *Harper's Magazine, 249*(1492), 23-30.

Haraway, D.J. (1991). *Simians, cyborgs, and women: The reinvention of nature*. New York: Routledge, Chapman & Hall.

Hayles, K. (2000). Visualizing the posthuman. *Art Journal, 59*(3), 50-54.

Heinlein, R.A. (1997). *The moon is a harsh mistress*. New York: Tom Doherty Associates.

Mayeroff, M. (1971). *On caring*. New York: Harper Perennial.

Moravec, H. (1999). *Robot: Mere machine to transcendent mind*. New York: Oxford University Press.

Newman, M.A. (1994). *Health as expanding consciousness* (2nd ed.). Boston: Jones & Bartlett.

Newman, M.A., Sime, A.M., & Corcoran-Perry, S.A. (1991). The focus of the discipline of nursing. *Advances in Nursing Science, 14*(1), 1-6.

Parse, R. (1993). Human becoming: Parse's theory of nursing. *Nursing Science Quarterly, 2,* 35-42.

Pollock, J. (1991). *How to build a person.* Cambridge, MA: The MIT Press.

Principa Cybernetica Web. (n.d.). *Cybernetics.* Retrieved August 15, 2003, from http://pespmc1.vub.ac.be/ASC/CYBERNETICS.html

Roach, M.S. (2002). *Caring, the human mode of being.* Ottowa, Ontario, Canada: CHA Press.

Rogers, M. (1970). *Introduction to the theoretical basis of nursing.* New York: F.A. Davis.

Roy, S., & Corliss, C. (1993). The Roy adaptation model: Theoretical update and knowledge for practice. In M. Parker (Ed.), *Patterns of nursing theories in practice* (pp. 215-229). New York: National League for Nursing.

Tudge, C. (1996). The future evolution of homo sapiens. *Earth, 5*(1), 36-40.

Turing, A.M. (1950). Computing machinery and intelligence. *Mind, 59*(256), 433-460.

Watson, J. (1999). *Nursing: Human science and human care.* New York: Jones & Bartlett.

Wiedenbach, E. (1984). *Nursing: A helping art.* New York: Springer.

" ... The concept of human beings as "whole in the moment" is intriguing. It does not really mean that human beings become incomplete in the next moment. Rather, it denotes that completeness or wholeness is expressed moment to moment ... "

10

CHAPTER

Vignettes of Caring: Stories and Reflective Summaries of Knowing

By Rozzano C. Locsin

Persons as Whole in the Moment

Vignette 1: Excerpted from "The Octopus in the Critical Care Setting: A Reflective Metaphorical Vision of Nursing," *by Marilyn S. Juergens, RN, BSN* (Personal communication.)

The early years of my 25 years of nursing were practiced in the medical-surgical setting. Becoming a critical care nurse was my dream. One day, on hearing this interest, the nursing supervisor on duty immediately took me for a tour in the 24-bed critical care unit of the hospital where I work. Before the end of the shift, I was informed that I had the job and to start orientation in the critical care unit soon. This change happened so fast. It was very exciting.

However, the clinical setting was more intense than what I was used to. The patients were very ill with multi-system problems. The immediate bedside set-up looked unfamiliar and complex. During orientation we had hands on and return demonstration on how to use certain machines and devices. The atmosphere was interesting yet overwhelming.

This experience brought on a new challenge. One certainty was the realization that as a nurse I felt nervous in unfamiliar places, around unfamiliar people, dealing with unfamiliar things, and in unfamiliar situations, the possibility is great that likewise, patients or any healthcare client will also be nervous when exposed to all these unfamiliar situations and conditions.

My experience in critical care nursing continued to grow. Every day brought a different challenge. I positioned myself as one among those on the frontline of critical care unit nurses within the hospital. The 24-bed unit increased to 32 beds. Renovation of the entire unit eventually happened. My role as a staff nurse expanded to being a resource nurse, a preceptor, and a substitute unit coordinator. Among all these roles, my preference was still primary patient care.

Through the years, I learned a lot and gained so much experience in caring for patients whose condition required they be in the critical care unit. Even with the increasing patient acuity and demands in staffing, I believed critical care nursing was the ultimate field for me. I wished to work nowhere else but the critical care area. I had no plans of moving to another field in nursing.

So, the puzzling question is, "Why did I leave the critical care unit?"

To some this is a mysterious question. It did not dawn on me that one day I would abandon the very area of practice I had always dreamed about. I was so much into patient care. I remember there were many times that I refused an assignment offer to be coordinator for the unit rather than give up patient care. There were times I did not want to be a preceptor either, and I instead asked to take care of the sickest patient in the unit. I gave excuses that I was always a preceptor and needed a break. This excuse made me feel guilty most of the time, because I knew that nurses new to critical care nursing needed support as much as I needed it when I was a novice in this department.

In my ambition to offer quality care to my patients, I call it "care plus quality," I did everything to give the best care possible. When I was assigned to someone very ill, I welcomed the challenge. I was interested in learning about new trends. When new technology was introduced, I adapted to it easily. I looked at it as a learning opportunity to improve patient care. This went on for 17 years. So many nurses in the unit came and went during this time. The nurse manager told me once that nurses averaged 10-12 years in critical care nursing. There were episodes when I felt some work-related frustrations, but a few days off took care of the problem. I never thought of leaving the critical care unit then. I was doing very well.

I continued to take care of the very sick patients in the unit. Naturally, those patients were the ones hooked up to all kinds of devices for all sorts of purposes: therapeutic, monitoring, diagnostic, and preventive. Some devices were used to support an ongoing study. Others were used for product evaluation. There were machines used as a last recourse and others for mechanical support, no longer life support.

I noticed the increasing responsibilities related to my job that directed me to the use of more machines than ever before. It used to be that an outside agency provided a technician to manage machines requiring high technology in the critical care unit—machines such as the intra-aortic balloon pump (IABP). Due to expensive service charges by the agency, this practice was stopped. A core group of critical care nurses were trained to run the IABP and to take care of the patient as well. This was a successful solution. I was one of the first 10 nurses trained in this hospital in this system, and it worked very well. On days when a patient needed the support of an IABP immediately, the trained nurse was available to operate the machine right away. This required instant flexibility to sudden changes in assignment. The patient might be in another section of the critical care unit, in the heart catheterization lab, in the operating room, or being transferred from another hospital. There was nothing to it. I took all of these demands in stride as required of specially trained critical care nurses.

However, a major turning point in my career came when I took care of a patient who had cardiomyopathy. He was in his early fifties, needed a heart transplant, was critically ill, and was physiologically very unstable. He was on a respirator, had all kinds of devices and multiple catheters attached to his body and extremities. He had a device called the LVAD (Left Ventricular Assistive Device). All critical care nurses were given a course on taking care of patients with LVAD. Large tubes were attached to his chest. He received more than one hundred units of blood products. Multiple emergency medications and liters of fluid were administered to him. Every day of his confinement he was rushed to the operating room. One by one, his body systems failed. There was no sign that his body responded positively to everything done to him. Eventually we lost him, although from the beginning he was not expected to live long. It is unimaginable how the patient and his family perceived the whole situation. The patient no longer looked like he did when he arrived. When I looked at him I thought, "What have we done to this man?"

From that moment on, my perspective changed. I felt that working around so many machines was pulling me away from nursing. The focus in patient care was shifting so that I was afraid of becoming machine/procedure centered, rather than patient-centered. The force behind advancing technology was so strong that I feared I would be engulfed by it. This was unfortunate, but I wanted out. My decision to leave the critical care unit was really powered by my search for something else: caring and nursing, not operating machines. When I was told I had been scheduled for training to do continuous dialysis, I protested quietly. I knew my time had come to say good-bye to ICU-CCU.

Leaving the critical care unit was my silent declaration that I did not want to deal with another device, button, switch, or other parts of machines that come into contact with patients in order to deliver "care plus quality" patient care. Please forgive my analogy, but when all kinds of tubes and hoses are hooked up to my patients, an octopus comes to my mind. Its tentacles are obstructing my way. I used to ask myself, "Where is the patient for whose care I am entrusted?" (Juergens, 2001. personal communication.)

Reflections on Clinical Experiences

Vignette 2: Reflecting on Mr. K's Care, *by Meg Goddard*

The following vignette is a reflective summary about the care that Mr. K received and the learning opportunities provided by the experience. Using the four ways of knowing as guide—empirical, aesthetic, ethical, and personal knowledge (Carper, 1978)—the care of the person is re-lived anew. This reflective summary is a requirement in the course "Nursing Situations in Acute Care Settings." Permission was obtained from Ms. Marion Goddard to publish an edited version of the summary.

Personal Knowing:

I was delighted to see that Mr. K was my assigned patient for this clinical day. He had been my patient last week, and I felt bad that I had not been able to talk to him very much. Since Mr. K had been short of breath and lethargic last week, our conversations were limited. Because of his diagnosis of pneumonia, I knew that it was in his best interest to rest. I knew that his shortness of breath was also due to his heart failure. My personal knowing in this nursing situation was enhanced because of my previous experience caring for Mr. K. I knew that simply being present with him was a significant way to express my caring. I also realized that being busy performing tasks can become a distraction from caring for our patients.

I was also able to draw upon my experience of caring for two elderly friends who had developed congestive heart failure. One was an 85 year-old woman who was a widow and lived alone. Her doctors had prescribed digoxin, furosemide, and potassium chloride to treat her condition. She was very confused about her medications, so I made sure she took the correct amount at the correct time. Another dear friend and neighbor also needed my assistance to administer her medications when she developed heart failure. She too was a widow who had no children and, at age 87, had difficulty with medication compliance. Being familiar with the medications that my friends had taken and witnessing their recovery was helpful in my experience of caring for Mr. K.

The first thing I noticed about Mr. K was the improvement in his breathing. He was no longer short of breath and was more talkative than the previous week. His first request of the day was to be fed. Even though his chest X-ray had revealed a worsening of the opacities in his lungs, Mr. K appeared slightly less pale and he was no longer coughing as much as the week before. When the occupational therapist arrived, she instructed him to perform as much of his own bathing as possible. Again, I was surprised by his improved strength and stamina. When I finished bathing Mr. K, I massaged his feet and legs with lotion. His wife arrived at this time and she kidded me about spoiling her husband. Mr. K smiled and nodded his head in agreement. She told me how meticulous he was when it came to bathing, and she told me how much she appreciated the wonderful care I was providing her husband. Seeing Mr. K smile and knowing that even a simple foot massage would mean so much to my patient made me feel happy. He drifted off to sleep for almost an hour. I felt at peace just watching my patient rest. I know that competence is a vital part of nursing, but I am now even more aware of how the simplest act of caring can enhance a person's state of well-being.

Empirical Knowing:

Mr. K is a 75 year old male admitted on December 31, 2002. His diagnosis is congestive heart failure. His past medical history includes pneumonia, coronary artery bypass graft, hyperlipidemia, non-insulin dependent diabetes mellitus, bladder cancer, lung cancer, atrial fibrillation, hypertension, left hip surgery, and peripheral vascular disease.

His vital signs are: BP: 120/73, pulse: 83 and irregular, temperature 97.7, respiration 20, oxygen saturation: 92% with 2L.

Here is a listing of his test results and current medications:

- Abnormal labs: Na: 128 L; Glu:343 H; BUN: 56 H; Creatinine: 1.9 H; Chloride: 91 L; Protime PT: 25. 7; INR: 4. 1
- Chest x-ray performed January 19, revealed a worsening of diffuse pulmonary opacities bilaterally.
- Medications:
  - Simvastatin (Zocor), dose: 20mg, PO, qd for management of hypercholesterolemia and reduction of lipids.
  - Spironolactone (Aldactone), dose: 25 mg, qd, PO for management of heart failure.
  - Insulin, regular human (Humulin R), SUBQ, q6hr—dose determined by sliding scale for management of diabetes mellitus. Used to control blood sugar.
  - Digoxin (Lanoxin 0. 5 mg/2ml INJ), dose: 0.125mg, IV. IV administration should be more than five minutes at least. Monitor apical pulse for 1 minute before administering and withhold if rate is <60bpm. For treatment of congestive heart failure and atrial fibrillation.
  - Potassium Chloride (K-Dur 20MEQ tablet), dose: 20 MEQ, bid, PO. For treatment or prevention of potassium depletion.
  - Torsemide (Demadex 50mg/5ml AMP), dose 40mg, q12hr, IV. For management of edema secondary to congestive heart failure.
  - Amiodarone HCL (Cordarone 200mg), dose: 400mg, bid, PO. For management and prophylaxis of life-threatening ventricular arrhythmias.
  - Choice DM Nutritional Supplement, tid, to supplement regular diabetic diet.

- Dextrose 5% Water IV solution.

- Milrinone Lactate (Primacor 1mg/ml vial), concentration = 200mcg/ml. Indicated for short-term treatment of congestive heart failure unresponsive to conventional therapy with digitalis glycosides, diuretics, and vasodilators.

- Acetaminophen (Tylenol extra strength 500mg), dose: 1000mg, q4hr, PO. For pain and fever.

- Choice DM nutritional supplement tid.

- Physical Assessment:

  - Neurologic: alert and oriented, slightly lethargic.

  - Skin: pale, cool, and dry. Purpura seen on right and left upper extremities. Stage 2 ulcer over the lower sacrum covered by Duoderm bandage. One inch area of redness across the bridge of the nose noted. Skin thin with elastic turgor.

  - Head: normocephalic, symmetric, hair is thin and grey.

  - Eyes: pupils equal, round, and react to light.

  - Mouth: mucosa pale, lips chapped.

  - Nose: mucous membranes moist and pink, no discharge.

  - Lungs: bibasilar crackles. No wheezes or rhonchi.

  - Heart and peripheral vascular system: systolic murmur heard loudest at S2. No edema noted. Pulses 2+ bilaterally. No bruits noted.

  - Musculoskeletal: muscle atrophy and weakness. Limited range of motion in left hip.

  - Abdomen: soft and nontender. Bowel sound in all four quadrants.

Description of Dependent Nursing Activities:

Mr. K continues to receive Digoxin to improve cardiac output by increasing myocardial contractility and by slowing his heart rate. Since Mr. K's most recent chest x-ray indicates that his congestive heart failure is worsening, Milrinone (Primacor) and Spironolactone have been added to his therapeutic regimen. Milrinone is indicated for short-term therapy of congestive heart failure unresponsive to conventional therapy with digitalis glycosides, diuretics, and vasodilators. It is classified as an inotropic pharmaceutical. Inotropics increase myocardial contractility. Milrinone also decreases preload and afterload due to its dilating effect on vascular smooth muscle. Spironolactone is a potassium sparing diuretic but one of its newer uses is the treatment of congestive heart failure. Its mechanism of action is to inhibit aldosterone causing the body to excrete sodium and retain potassium. The excretion of sodium will help alleviate the edema. Furosemide has been replaced with torsemide. Torsemide is a loop diuretic. Its action is to inhibit sodium and chloride reabsorption in the Loop of Henle. Even though Mr. K's potassium levels fall within the normal range, potassium chloride has been prescribed as a preventative measure. Potassium supplements are also indicated for Mr. K because he takes insulin. Insulin causes the cells to take in potassium which may lead to hypokalemia. Amiodarone, a potassium blocker, is an antidysrhythmic drug that has been prescribed to control Mr. K's atrial fibrillation. His BUN has increased from 38 to 56. This could be an indication of dehydration.

> What bothered me most about this situation was the fact that no one had taken the time to ask Mr. K why he had become angry.

The intake and output from the previous day indicated that Mr. K's fluid balance was -703. His creatinine level is high at 1.9. This indicates impairment of renal function related to congestive heart failure. The medications used to improve cardiac output like Digoxin and Milrinone will help his kidneys by enhancing blood perfusion in his renal system. Aside from the order for Choice DM, there was nothing in chart that indicated an intervention to increase this patient's fluid intake. Mr. K's chloride level was low because the diuretics are causing him to excrete more chloride.

Nursing diagnoses	Responses
Impaired gas exchange related to congestive heart failure.	Monitor respiratory and oxygenation status. Administer oxygen, as prescribed. Position patient to minimize respiratory effort. Monitor heart rate, rhythm, and pulses. Administer all prescribed, appropriate medications.
Decreased cardiac output due to congestive heart medications.	Administer all prescribed, appropriate medications. Be alert for digitalis toxicity failure, such as fatigue, anorexia, and mental status changes. Monitor intake and output and daily weights.
Activity intolerance due to congestive heart failure.	Provide physical and emotional rest. Allow patient to sit in chair and perform leg exercises.
Impaired skin integrity as evidenced by stage two ulcers due to impaired tissue perfusion and lack of adequate nutrition.	Apply protective barriers to ulcer on sacrum. Supply adequate nutrition. Reposition patient q2hr.

Ethical knowing:

When I arrived in Mr. K's room, I noticed a large pool of water beneath his bed. I asked a person from the housekeeping department to please come to the room to dry the area. During report, I learned that Mr. K. had become angry and threw a pitcher of water at a patient-care assistant. The nurse giving report guessed that he had become frustrated. No one was injured by this incident. The water stayed on the floor until I mopped it up.

What bothered me most about this situation was the fact that no one had taken the time to ask Mr. K. why he had become angry. I know his anger did not justify throwing something at another person. I am aware that nurses should not tolerate abuse by their patients, but I do feel that we have a responsibility to communicate with our patients. If a patient is frustrated with the hospital staff, it seems to be a good idea to allow the patient the opportunity to voice his frustrations. Preventing an incident such as this one would be in everyone's best interest. When patients become abusive, are they not informed that their behavior is inappropriate and unacceptable and will not be tolerated? When I was shoved by a patient last semester, her doctor told her to stop being abusive or she would be sent to jail. I wondered if that was the best approach to calm an angry patient. I never found out whether the patient stopped shoving people. How to handle abusive patients is an issue worth exploring. I will plan to research it.

Aesthetic Knowing

Vignette 3: Reflecting on Mr. S, *by Loren Nedelman.*

Following is the reflective summary about the care that Mr. S received, and the learning opportunities provided by the experience. Using the four ways of knowing as guide, the care of the person is re-lived anew. This reflective summary is a requirement in the course "Nursing Situations in Acute Care Settings." Permission was obtained from Mr. Loren Nedelman to publish an edited version of the summary.

> What if he is found to be free of any mental deficits and doesn't want some type of care being offered?

Personal Knowing:

My patient this past week was a 74 year old male with no religious preference. He was admitted on February 2 with the medical diagnosis of cardiomyopathy, probably due to conduction system disease or coronary artery disease. Mr. S had an intra-cardiac defibrillator (ICD) placed the next day. He was originally from Pennsylvania, lives with his wife, and sold tools for a living. As I introduced myself, I asked him what I could do for him to feel better today, and I conducted my assessment. He stated he felt pretty good and there was not a lot he really needed. I offered to him help with morning care, which he accepted. He thanked me, as he did feel my caring had helped him. And, although he stated he wasn't very hungry, I insisted he try and eat something, and he saw this as another sign of my caring—not giving up on him but enforcing his well-being. His body needed nourishment especially if he was to go back into surgery to complete the placing of his ICD, which had a lead that had not been placed in one of the ventricles. His doctor wanted to put the lead in to get better capture by the ICD. There was some indication that he had a historical event of a "brain attack" which affected his right hemisphere and possibly the reasoning areas of his brain. I did not find much residual sign of this in my limited assessment, and during our conversations he seemed only somewhat forgetful at times, something which most elderly persons have normally.

I did not understand ethically why the doctors had not properly placed his ICD the first time. Why put this man through another surgery? Did they just hurry up and throw it into his chest or did it just come out of position? I also wondered, if they did believe he had some cognitive changes, why was it not properly addressed. Mr. S's wife stated many times during conversations with me and the physician that her husband had a stroke and it may be affecting him.

I guess when I am the nurse I will need to have this addressed properly. What if he is found to be free of any mental deficits and doesn't want some type of care being offered? Should we listen to him or his wife?

Empirical Knowing:

- Medications
  - Lisinopril (Zestril), an ACE inhibitor used to control hypertension by breaking the angiotension I conversion into angiotension II, which acts to vasoconstrict blood vessels and thus increasing SVR, more work on the heart.
  - Potassium (K-Dur), an electrolyte used to replace potassium excreted due to the use of a diuretic.
  - Furosemide (Lasix), used to help lower blood pressure by decreasing the amount of fluid filling the heart and thereby making it work more efficiently.
  - Metoprolol (Lopressor), used for hypertension and to manage heart failure due to the patient's cardiomyopathy. It works by blocking the stimulation of beta1 receptor sites, thus decreasing heart rate and allowing vasodilation.
  - Levofloxacin (Levaquin), used as a prophylaxis against infection after patient's pacemaker implantation surgery.
  - Cephalexin (Keflex), used as a prophylaxis against infection after patient's pacemaker implantation surgery.
  - Heparin, used to prevent blood clots due to ECG monitor A-FIB, and post-op prophylaxis.

- Physical Assessment:
  - T: 975F PO, P-79, B/P 119/76, R-16, SPo2-96%
  - H: A&O x3 but has some forgetfulness. Able to follow simple commands.
  - E: PERRAL, wears glasses, pupil size 2-3mm bilat.
  - E: Appears normal; no internal visualization performed, able to comprehend whisper.
  - N: Nasal Cannula in place, breathing through nose in no apparent distress.

- T: on cardiac diet; tolerating well; no lymphadenopthy noted.
- L: bilat clear, slightly decreased at bases. On 2L NC.
- Abd: bowel sounds noted in all quads, non-tender, 10mm scar, midline lower quads noted. Pt has not had bowel movement since yesterday.
- CV: S1/S2 heard, cap refill 2-3 sec, skin pink, warm, and moist; pedal pulses +1 bilat, radial pulses +2 bilat; ECG reading Lead II A-fib with pacer spikes noted. Pt denies any chest pain or any signs of defibrillator discharge; left arm in sling to decrease movement; midline of thorax with approx 16mm scar from past CABG.
- GU: Foley cath with yellow urine draining approx 60cc/hr.
- MS: able to turn side to side, back with no signs of redness or pain; bilat strength noted in upper extremities; lower are slightly weaker.

- Labs:
  - All WNL except noted: PTT-49; Heparin infusion caused elevation.
  - PT-13. 9: recent use of coumadin elevation.
  - Bun-30: elevation due to probable muscle breakdown from surgery, kidney disease, dehydration.
  - Cre-1. 7: elevated probably due to kidney disease or dysfunction.

- Nursing Diagnoses:
  - Self care deficit; R/T arm immobilized AEB assistance needed for ADL.
  - Risk of decreased cardiac output; R/T cardiomyopathy AEB decreased stroke volume.
  - Risk for decreased activity; R/T cardiac output AEB; needing assistance to get out of bed.

Aesthetic Expression

Using a heart that was painted on paper caused a reflective understanding of the intricacies of an organ system, initially attributed to be the central case of being human. As an aesthetic project, such illustration shows the heart as the main focus of my patient's illness that sent shock waves from the defibrillator put in and of the miscommunication of his own heart's electrical system.

Answering Calls for Nursing

Vignette 4: Reflecting on Mr. M's Care, by Loren Nedelman

Following is a reflective summary about the care that Mr. M received and the learning opportunities provided by this experience. Using the four ways of knowing as a guide, the care of this person is re-lived anew. This reflective summary is a requirement for the course "Nursing Situations in Acute Care Settings." Permission was obtained from Mr. Loren Nedelman to publish an edited version of the summary.

My patient this week was a 74 year old male of the Christian faith. He was admitted on February 18, 2003, with the medical diagnosis of chest pain, which turned out to be caused by an inferior wall MI. Mr. M lives with his wife and has a "great" relationship with his neighbor, who helps him out often, and Mr. M in turn repays with his help. As I introduced myself upon arrival, I asked him what I could do for him to feel better today, and I conducted my assessment. He stated he felt pretty good and there was not a lot he really needed. I offered him help with morning care, which he accepted. He thanked me as he did feel my caring had helped him. He noted that none of the other staff had even bothered to offer him a toothbrush. This effort from me made him feel even better, and he knew I really was trying to care. As I was assessing him and his environment, I noticed the room was very hot and humid, and he had on two different types of shoes and a gardening glove on his right hand. I knew this might not be normal behavior.

I knew I had an ethical call to ask him about this apparent abnormal behavior. I am glad I did get to know him and answer this ethical call. It turns out he had a neuropathy from a CVA which he had several years prior, and his right side extremities always felt cold. He forgot to take his left shoe off, and that is why he had two different shoes on. The glove he wore was to help his hand stay warm or give him the sensation of being warm due to his nerves not transmitting signals to the brain the way they used to.

I also had a chance to speak with his wife who seemed very anxious and worried. I asked what the doctor had told her about her husband. She said "the doctor told me his heart was clogged again." I explained that it appeared he had a heart attack from the elevated enzymes in his body and his EKG had some changes as well. She seemed a little bit at ease since I explained to her what was happening and took the time to be with them even though it was only for the moment.

> I knew I had an ethical call to ask him about this apparent abnormal behavior.

Empirical Knowing:

- Medications:
  - Nitroglycerin (Nitro-Bid), used to relieve any pain he might have from his myocardium not oxygenating and to reduce the preload and thus the strain on the heart.
  - Acetylsalicylic acid (Aspirin), used to decrease the coagulation cascade and avert the chance of blocking an artery.
  - Famotidine (Pepcid), used to help decrease stomach acid.
  - Clopidogrel (Plavix), used to reduce platelet aggregation and thereby hopefully avoid another atherosclerotic event (i.e. MI, stroke).
  - Enalapril Maleate (Vasotec), used to help with controlling hypertension and to rebuild and attempt to restore normal function of the myocardium.

- Physical Assessment:
  - T: 985F PO, P-60, B/P 152/72, R-16, SPo2-96%.
  - H: A&O x3; able to follow simple commands; has feeling of cold on right side of body.
  - E: PERRAL; wears glasses; pupil size 2-3mm bilateral.
  - E: appears normal; no internal visualization performed; able to comprehend whisper.
  - N: breathing through nose in no apparent distress.
  - T: on cardiac diet; tolerating well; no lymphadenopthy noted.
  - L: bilateral clear, slightly decreased at bases; on RA.
  - Abdomen: bowel sounds noted in all quads; non-tender; has had two bowel movements since yesterday; hard, formed, large amount brown stool.
  - CV: S1/S2 heard; cap refill 2-3 sec; skin pink, warm, and moist; pulses +2 bilat
  - ECG reading Lead II SR to sinus brady; Pt denies any chest pain.
  - GU: Voiding on own; yellowish urine.
  - MS: able to turn side to side, back with no signs of redness or pain; bilat strong; strength noted in extremities; left foot with yellowish-black ecchymosis noted to dorsal aspect of foot; Pt states a ladder caused the ecchymosis a few days prior to admission.

- Laboratory:
  - All WNL except noted: CPK-448 Elevated, CK-MB-64. 2-Elevated, Troponin-8. 51-Elevated.
  - All of the above labs are elevated due to muscle breakdown/ death, especially the myocardium specific of the troponin elevation.

- Nursing Diagnosis:
  1. Decreased cardiac output R/T MI AEB Elevated cardiac enzymes and EKG alterations.
  2. Risk for decreased activity R/T Cardiac Output AEB SOB upon minimal exertion.

Summary

A critical concept of the model of technological competency as caring is the idea of human beings as whole and complete in the moment. The concept of human beings as whole may not be a revolutionary thought. After all, it is commonly understood, particularly in a clinical sense, that a person is a thinking, sensual human being with a head, a body, two arms, two legs, and all the other physical aspects of a "normal" human being. However, what happens when the human being or person does not reflect or resemble the aforementioned human being? What happens when the being has some characteristics or composing features of a common human being? Think of Robin Williams' character in the movie, *The Bicentennial Man* as he strives to seek consideration and appreciation of his humanness because he is partly human and partly machine.

In reality, today, there are persons whose human bodies have electronic and mechanical composites such as parts of their cardiac and neurological systems: a mitral valve and pacemaker, an insulin pump, or a genetic-engineered pancreas. Nevertheless, the concept of human beings as "whole in the moment" is intriguing. It does not really mean that human beings become incomplete in

> The concept of human beings as "whole in the moment" is intriguing. It does not really mean that human beings become incomplete in the next moment. Rather, it denotes that completeness or wholeness is expressed moment to moment.

the next moment. Rather, it denotes that completeness or wholeness is expressed moment to moment, a phenomenon that sanctions the conception of nursing as the continuous "knowing of persons."

Similarly, completeness or wholeness does not necessarily mean "having been completed," or "being completed," wherein the intention is to understand a situational summation of a human being. "Whole in the moment" is the expression of being human moment to moment, wholeness of a person that declares the person as not needing any fixing or being made whole again. The supposition is that human beings are unpredictable, ever-changing, dynamic, and living. Therefore, as such, human beings can only be appreciated as in the moment, and, conditionally, only when she or he allows another (the nurse) to enter her or his world to know, affirm, celebrate, and support her or him as a caring person (Boykin & Schoenhofer, 2001).

However, the situation of completeness reflecting the summation of human parts is still popularized by the appreciation of clinical health (Smith, 1983), and it continues to gain practical understanding. Advancing technologies in genetics, inter-species creations, mechanized humans, combined robo-sapiens and techno-sapiens, and the eventual post human, altogether demand the redefinition of the concept of human beings as person.

The chapters within this section should engage the reader's imagination toward the consideration of human beings who are continuously evolving, furthering human evolution, perhaps toward the post human. How will the practice of nursing as knowing persons engage future human beings through caring in nursing, all the while recognizing the limited form and function of being human in the creation of opportunities of care that are illustrated as calls for nursing and responses of nursing?

References

Boykin, A., and Schoenhofer, S. (2001). *Nursing as Caring: A model for transforming practice*. Sudbury, CT: Jones and Bartlett.

Carper, B. (1978). Fundamental patterns of knowing in nursing. *Advances in Nursing Science, 1*(1), 13-23.

> "Cultures, health beliefs, and ways of being are embedded in genetics and heredity and should be assessed in order to appreciate the patient as a whole and integrated human being."

11

CHAPTER

The Technology of Genetics and Nursing

By Ruth McCaffrey

The Role of the Nurse in Genetics

Genetics is an exploding field of science spurred by new understandings of the human genome that is prompting the development of new technologies to prevent and cure disease. There is an awakening appreciation among medical scientists that the success or failure of every physiologic function in the human being depends on the orchestrated operation of hundreds of genes in concerted action (Hazzard, et al. 2003).

Every healthcare problem except for those caused by trauma has a genetic base (Collins, 1996). As genetic knowledge and genetically-based therapies and technologies are developed, healthcare providers may view persons as genetic blueprints rather than unique, integrated beings. Genetics as the science of heredity, establishes a link between each person and her or his ancestors. People's lives are profoundly affected by their genetic inheritance.

How does knowledge of genetics influence our understanding and practice of nursing now and in the future? What are the specific challenges that nurse's face as patient advocates, educators, and care givers as new genetic technologies for diagnoses and treatments of diseases are developed. Can we as nurses maintain our view of persons as integrated and whole and not simply the sum of their genetic blueprint? Does this new explosion of scientific knowledge affect the theoretical base of nursing philosophy? In order to answer these questions, the science of genetics must be explored from the view of science and technology, and also—in order to understand the societal and ethical impact genetic knowledge presents to patients—from the viewpoint of families and communities.

Nurses focus not only on the physical aspects of a person, but rather on the whole human being as more then the sum of her or his parts. The study of genetics raises many ethical, social policy, and legal questions. The birth of a long awaited child who is not a perfectly functioning human being causes families to face not only physical but psychosocial issues. The persecution or demeaning of a group because of their genetics, for example Jews in Germany during World War II or Blacks in the United States, is a social issue with moral, ethical, and legal components. Therefore, while we cannot fully understand a human being based on their genetic blueprint, the blueprint affects who we are and how others perceive us. Understanding genetic inheritance is part of understanding the uniqueness of each person.

Assessment is an integral part of the nursing process. Obtaining each person's genetic inheritance pattern has become a standard part of the nursing assessment. Cultures, health beliefs, and ways of being are embedded in genetics and heredity and should be assessed in order to appreciate the patient as a whole and integrated human being. Understanding the person's genetic history assists the nurse in seeing the effects of generations past.

Genetic assessment includes the development of a pedigree. A pedigree is a pictorial representation or diagram of a family history. Visually laying out the information obtained from the family history in a pedigree provides a representation of the person's relationship to affected individuals and may pinpoint any vital persons who should be examined or tested. Drawing a patient's pedigree can assist the nurse in understanding the pattern of inheritance (recessive, dominant, or X linked). Pedigree drawings may also be useful when educating patients and families about the inheritance of diseases.

> "Nurses, as patient advocates, need to be at the forefront of discussions about how to integrate genetic technology equitably and how to prevent genetic-based discrimination."

Symbols used for drawing pedigrees have been standardized, and there are computer programs that will assist in pedigree development. Figure 11.1 is an example of the symbols used to prepare a pedigree. Figure 11.2 depicts a human pedigree.

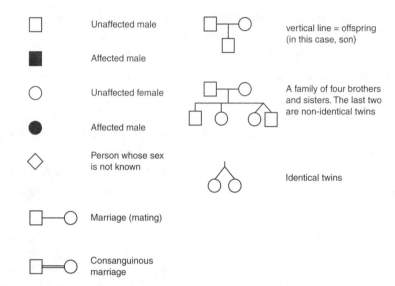

Figure 11.1 *Examples of the symbols used to prepare a genetic pedigree.*

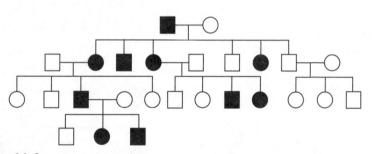

Figure 11.2 *A human pedigree*

Educating patients about their genetic history and helping them to understand how genetics influences health has become a standard part of the nursing plan of care and goals for each patient. Genetic scientists will eventually present the nurse with an opportunity to provide life-long health promotion, disease prevention, education, and treatments based on the patient's specific genetic make-up. Genetic discoveries are frequently published in the news media before the tests or treatments representing the potential of those discoveries are available to the public. This causes patients to ask nurses when these genetic tests and treatments might become commercially available. Staying informed will allow nurses to provide important information at the appropriate time for patients and families.

While many benefits are provided through increased genetic knowledge, many challenges are also presented. The science of genetics has outstripped the ability of society to adapt new rules and ethical standards for the implementation of this new scientific knowledge. Cloning is a genetic technology that is currently available but ethically and morally undesirable to many in our society. Many questions exist about who should receive genetic testing. Just a few of these questions are: Should genetic testing be mandatory or voluntary? And, how should the information be used?

Nurses, as patient advocates, need to be at the forefront of discussions about how to integrate genetic technology equitably and how to prevent genetic-based discrimination. In 1994, the Institute of Medicine (IOM) predicted that nurses would play a critical role in providing genetic information and services to patients, families, and communities (Andrews et. al., 1994). Further, nurses must be able to provide ethical and legal information, guidance, and understanding of social issues surrounding genetic diagnosis, testing, and screening.

The American Nurses Association (ANA) (1998) has prepared the Statement on the Scope and Standards of Genetics Clinical Nursing Practice as a guideline for nurses. This guide indicates that all nurses have a role in the delivery of genetics services and the management of genetic information. Nurses are responsible for the health of those for whom they care, and genetic knowledge affects the health of persons in many ways. As nurses become more comfortable with genetic knowledge and understand genetic diseases, testing, and treatments, they will be challenged to address patient concerns. These include emotional concerns related to the discovery of genetic conditions; ethical, legal, and social issues about the disclosure of genetic information; and health education about genetics and informed decision making regarding genetic testing and treatments. Other issues that nurses will address concerning genetic information are patient self-image and self-esteem, assisting patients to cope with the knowledge regarding their risk for genetic diseases, and incorporating this knowledge into their daily lives.

In contrast to many healthcare groups, most nurses consider themselves genetically uneducated. At the 2002 ANA convention, attendees were questioned to determine if they felt they had an adequate knowledge of genetics. Mores than half of those in attendance said they were not competent enough to provide care that involved genetics (Jenkins & Collins, 2003). Therefore, in order to increase genetic competence among nurses, it seems important to develop genetic education programs at all levels of nursing education. The National Coalition for Health Professional Education in Genetics has provided recommendations of educational objectives that all healthcare professionals should be able to meet (see Table 11.1).

With the completion of the human genome project, genetic treatments and testing will become a common part of American healthcare. In 1999, the ANA House of Delegates stated that nurses should have a strong knowledge base in genetics to be able to assess patients regarding genetic disorders and to provide genetic information and referrals. The ANA agreed to:

- Promote the inclusion of information about genetics in basic, advanced, and continuing education programs.

- Promote dissemination of information about genetic discoveries and their applications in healthcare.

- Advocate for non-discrimination toward persons and families with a risk for a condition with a genetic component.

- Study ethical and practical implications of genetics development.

The nursing process is consistent with nurse's genetic practice. Assessment collects data and identifies patient needs for education. The assessment identifies calls for nursing care, educational needs, goal setting, and needs for referrals. Data must be collected with confidentiality in mind. Ethical issues include informed consent before assessment or testing is undertaken, truth telling, disclosure, privacy, and non-discrimination.

The identification of risk factors associated with genetic inheritance is the focus of the nursing diagnosis. This type of risk assessment must be carried out in an ethical manner, especially regarding confidentiality. In many cases, the consideration of a genetic cause for disease is new information for family members, and a thorough explanation is required to help them understand and adjust to this information.

Expected outcomes come after diagnosis and are formulated by the nurse, the patient, and any other family members who are appropriate after making a genetically-based diagnosis. Developing an understanding of the patient's needs and desires is essential to the development of outcomes that will be acceptable. During outcome development, nurses need to be authentically present with patients and families in order to identify calls for nursing care surrounding genetic testing and treatments. The inclusion of an interdisciplinary team may be needed to provide information regarding all aspects of genetic testing and treatment. Nurses should ensure that outcomes are developed using the current scientific knowledge in clinical genetics.

> "Nurses should be able to identify individuals, families, groups, or communities at risk for genetic conditions."

An individualized plan of care for the patient and family is tailored to the client's genetic needs and desires. Mutually identified goals using specific interventions based on genetic principles are essential. Consultation, referral, and follow-up are important aspects of the plan that the nurse, patient, and family develop. As with all other aspects of the nursing plan of care, awareness of ethical, legal, and social issues should be included in the plan. Interventions come from the plan of care and are based on the needs of the patient and family. All interventions should be evidence based using current genetic knowledge.

Nurses should be able to identify individuals, families, groups, or communities at risk for genetic conditions. Using markers such as advanced reproductive age, consanguinity, and family history to identify persons at risk for genetic diseases is within the scope of nursing practice. The ability to identify persons at risk comes from knowledge of genetic and nursing research and an awareness of and sensitivity to confidentiality and non-discrimination.

Nurses should provide genetic health education to persons for whom they care. The education should be founded on solid genetic principles, providing resources for further information, and at a level appropriate for the person. Genetic conditions, treatment options, risk reduction, and screening services should be explored as part of genetic patient information.

The International Society of Nurses in Genetics (ISONG) has developed a guideline for the preparation of advanced practice genetics nurses. Genetic counseling and case management are interventions performed by these nurses with advanced knowledge and skills. Genetic counselors specialize in areas of medical genetics and counseling. They usually work as members of a multidisciplinary team to offer information and support to families. Genetic counselors identify families at risk, investigate the problem in the family, interpret information about the disorder, analyze inheritance patterns, and review available options with the family. Genetic counseling is usually provided to women over 35 years old who are planning a pregnancy, including couples who are planning a pregnancy and have had a child with a genetic disorder, who have a first degree relative with a genetic disorder, for women who have experienced multiple miscarriages or who have had babies who died in infancy, and pregnant women who have had blood testing or ultrasound testing that shows a possible birth defect.

Advanced practice genetic nurses are able to construct a risk assessment for the family using all available information. Effective communication of the amount of risk for a couple contemplating pregnancy is a difficult task, however, it is a task that provides the couple with information that may be vital to their planed pregnancy.

Genetic screening is the systematic and organized search for individuals who have certain genotypes. Genetic screening begins in newborns for diseases such as phenylketonuria, galactosemia, congenital hypothyroidism, and hemoglobinopathies such as sickle cell and thalassemia. Table 11.2 lists the diseases that can now be diagnosed by pre-natal testing. Preconception screenings for potential parents with family histories of genetic abnormalities include Tay-Sachs, sickle cell, cystic fibrosis, and others. Some environmental factors can cause genetic diseases, and screening should be undertaken if these factors exist. These include diseases such as G6PD deficiency, thalassemia, erythrocyte porphyria, and gout.

Genetic screening and testing have provided benefits to individuals and society; however, these programs have also created problems and have raised ethical and social questions. Who should have access to this type of testing? Should this testing be mandatory? How can we prevent carriers of genetic defects from being stigmatized?

Personal consequences of being a carrier of a genetic disease can have a devastating psychological effect. Loss of self-esteem and a sense of decreased self worth often occur in these people. In some cultures, families with a known genetic disorder are shunned or considered not suitable as marriage partners. Genetic counseling provides these persons with options for preventing unwanted pregnancies and child bearing, including adoption, artificial insemination, and prenatal diagnosis coupled with selective abortion.

> A core value in nursing is truth telling. Genetic information provides nurses with new ethical challenges in the area of truth telling. It is not always simple to identify the "truth" in genetic terms because what is true today may not be true tomorrow.

Communities feel the social consequences of genetic testing and screening where large-scale genetic screening is mandated by governmental agencies. Voluntary rather than mandatory participation, coupled with adequate education and counseling and community involvement would foster a sense of self-determination in these communities. The National Institutes of Health (NIH) has recommended that certain screenings be made available to all newborns to avoid issues of ethnic and racial origin. Issues surrounding genetic screening, confidentiality of information, and the greater good of the public continue to be debated at many levels of society.

There are many legal implications surrounding genetic testing and screening. If a child is born with a genetic defect that could have been diagnosed pre-natally, can the healthcare provider be held responsible for not informing the parents that prenatal screening was available? Can insurers drop coverage for those patients who have a child with a genetic disorder who decide to have another child? Who can be told about a genetic condition once it has been diagnosed by either mandatory or voluntary screening? The issue of cloning and how other genetic technologies will be used in society is a major legal, ethical, and social hurtle to be overcome. All of these and other questions will have to be decided on a case-by-case basis and precedent will have to be set.

A core value in nursing is truth telling. Genetic information provides nurses with new ethical challenges in the area of truth telling. It is not always simple to identify the "truth" in genetic terms because what is true today may not be true tomorrow. When giving genetic information, nurses must tell patients how quickly the body of knowledge in genetics is evolving. Truth telling may be difficult when there are unexpected findings. When genetic testing discovers that the male who believes he is the father of a baby is not the biological father, is it ethical to tell the truth if the mother does not wish it?

Reviewing the ANA Code of Ethics with interpretive statements provides an overview of the nurse's ethical responsibility in the care rendered to patients and families receiving genetic services. Nurses, because of their distinct relationships with patients and their centrality in the provision of care, offer a unique perspective to understanding, assessing, and responding to ethical issues.

Genetics in Healthcare

Since the mapping of the human genome was completed in 2001, genes have been associated with the incidence and prevalence of many diseases. Knowledge of genetics has also increased understanding of how individuals respond to many drug therapies. Genetic treatments to prevent or cure many diseases are being explored. As news of this exciting knowledge and the possibilities offered by an understanding of genetics is reported, public expectation for new and better options for health promotion and disease prevention has grown. Despite the rapid pace of genetic discovery and the announcement of these discoveries to the public, clinical application of these discoveries has yet to be fully developed. A time lag exists between the discovery of genetic information and the ability to use this knowledge to provide clinical applications for disease modification.

One of the causes of the time lag between discovery and clinical application of genetic information comes from the lack of knowledge among nurses and other healthcare providers about the science of genetics and the technological improvements that are offered by this knowledge. Nurses are challenged to integrate new information about genetics into their clinical practice, develop appropriate interventions based on genetic information, and to help patients use genetic discoveries in a positive way (Williams, 2002).

In the 1970s, nurses began to function as genetic counselors. Newborn metabolic screening programs and prenatal diagnostic clinics were the first places genetics was routinely used to plan and care for patients. In the 1990s, genetic discoveries began to increase with the discovery of genes like BRCA1 and BRCA2 for familial breast cancer. These types of discoveries offered predictive genetic testing to women with strong family histories of breast cancer in order to provide early detection and treatment. Genetic factors associated with diseases such as cancer make it imperative that nurses have an understanding of genetics in order to properly care for and educate their patients.

ISONG has developed standards for educating nurses about genetics and competencies that should be required at various levels of nursing education. ISONG has further proposed that nurses at all practice levels should be able to collect and obtain genetic history information, offer genetic information to patients, and provide explanations of genetic resources (ISONG, 1998). All nurses must be able to participate in the informed consent and informed decision-making processes that are required for genetic counseling and treatments. Finally, all nurses should be knowledgeable about genetic treatments in order to manage patients who have a genetic component to their disease; monitor the impact of genetic conditions, testing, and treatments; and evaluate outcomes for the person and family.

History of Genetic Research and Discovery

The science of genetics dates back to the Middle Ages when Gregory Mendel, an Augustinian monk, discovered that crossbreeding flowering pea plants enabled him to identify distinguishing characteristics or traits that were passed from parent plants to their offspring. Even before that time, the Talmud and the Bible describe an understanding of basic genetics in plant and animal breeding. Today genetic biotechnological developments have produced fundamental changes in the diagnosis and treatment of disease. As the biological science of genetics has advanced, many ethical issues have arisen. Some of the unsolved ethical and legal questions include the idea of cloning, genetic profiling, and access to genetic information about individuals.

> The science of genetics dates back to the Middle Ages when Gregory Mendel, an Augustinian monk, discovered that crossbreeding flowering pea plants enabled him to identify distinguishing characteristics or traits that were passed from parent plants to their offspring.

The history of genetic knowledge in the United States begins in the 1950s when scientists discovered the correct number of chromosomes in humans and the structure of deoxyribonucleic acid (DNA). During this time the first truly genetic disease phenylketonuria (PKU), an excess accumulation of phenylalanine in the blood leading to mental retardation, was discovered. A low phenylalanine diet to treat PKU was instituted as the first genetic treatment.

The National Genetic Diseases Program was established in 1976 and is commonly known as the Genetic Diseases Act. This act established a national program to fund basic and applied research, training, testing, counselling, and information about genetic diseases such as Tay-Sachs, cystic fibrosis, Huntington's chorea, thalassemia, and muscular dystrophy. s

In the mid 1990s, the Human Genome Project was started. This was an effort by the National Center for Human Genome Research at the NIH to achieve the following goals:

- Genetic mapping.
- Physical mapping.
- Sequencing the three billion DNA base pairs of the human genome.
- Developing improved technology for genome analysis.
- Identifying all genes and their functions, especially those associated with disease.
- Identifying the genetic characteristics of nonhuman organisms such as Escherichia coli, a bacterium; *Drosophila melanogaster*, the fruit fly; and *Saccharomyces cerevisiae*, yeast.
- Undertaking a program to address the ethical, legal, and social implications of genetic research and their implications.
- Training of students and scientists.

Definition of Genetic Terms

A glossary is provided at the end of this chapter. The glossary will be helpful to reinforce the definition of terms as you learn about genetics. However, a few terms require more than a glossary definition.

A gene is a linear sequence of chemical building blocks called nucleotides in a DNA molecule that form the functional unit of heredity. The sequence of nucleotides in a DNA molecule stores information in the form of a genetic code. After the stored information is decoded in the cell, it is translated into a polypeptide, which is a molecule with a three-dimensional structure known as a protein. The action of these proteins produces genetic traits that are observable in humans. Genes can undergo replication as they are copied, mutation as they undergo change, expression as they are turned on and off, and recombination as they move from one chromosome to another.

> "Only 0.1% of our DNA makes us different from each other in skin color, facial features, stature, and physical ability"

A genome is the entire DNA in an organism. As humans, we share 75% of our DNA with a banana, and each human being has 99.9% of the same DNA (Cummings, 2000). Only 0.1% of our DNA makes us different from each other in skin color, facial features, stature, and physical ability (Cummings, 2000). The genome is a complete blueprint for an organism and all of the functions in the organism.

The map for the genome is constructed of tightly coiled threads of deoxyribonucleic acid (DNA). The DNA molecule is the largest molecule known to science. DNA is made up of four similar chemical bases; adenine (A), thymine (T), cytosine (C), and guanine (G). These are repeated millions or billions of times throughout a genome. Each base combines with only one other (called base pairing). For example, A only pairs with T and C only pairs with G in the opposite chain. The human genome, for example, has three billion base pairs. The particular order in which the bases occur is extremely important and underlies all of life's diversity, even dictating whether an organism is human or another species such as yeast, rice, or fruit fly. Because all organisms are related through similarities in DNA sequences, insights gained from nonhuman genomes often lead to new knowledge about human biology.

As noted, there are three billion base pairs in the human genome. Each of these base pairs is organized into one of 24 distinct, physically separate microscopic units called a chromosome. Genes are arranged linearly along the chromosomes. The nucleus of most human cells contains two sets of chromosomes, one from each parent. Each set of chromosomes has 23 single chromosomes. Twenty-two of these are autosomes (chromosomes that have a non-reproductive function). One of them is a sex chromosome—either an X or Y. A normal female has two X chromosomes and a normal male has one X and one Y chromosome. Chromosomes are made up equally of protein and DNA.

Phenotype is the outward expression of a genetic trait; for example, one person may express a green eye phenotype and a blue eye phenotype. Each gene has two alleles, one from each parent. If the phenotype comes from one parent only, the trait is said to be dominant; however, if the phenotype comes from both parents, the trait is said to be recessive.

Dominant traits require that every affected individual have at least one affected parent. When one parent has the dominant trait, there is a 50% chance of transmitting the trait to each child. If both parents have the dominant trait, it is still possible to have an unaffected child. Marfan syndrome, familial hypercholesterolemia, adult polycystic kidney disease, and Huntington's disease are examples of autonomic (non-sex linked) dominant diseases.

Recessive traits require that both parents contribute the trait in order for the child to express the trait in their phenotype. All of the children of two recessive parents will be affected. Cystic Fibrosis, Phenylketonuria, sickle cell anemia and Tay-Sachs disease are examples of autosomal (non-sex linked) recessive diseases.

Sex-linked inheritance involves genes on the X and Y-chromosomes. Females have two X chromosomes, and males have one X and one Y chromosome. The genes on the X chromosome are not present on the Y chromosome, and this causes the pattern of transmission known as sex-linked inheritance. Males transmit their X chromosome to all daughters and their Y chromosome to their sons. Therefore, if a genetic trait is X-linked, males pass this to all of their daughters. X-linked diseases have dominant and recessive forms of inheritance. In an X-linked dominant disease, affected males produce all affected daughters and no affected sons. Fifty percent of children of a mother with an X-linked dominant trait will have the disease. For diseases that are X-linked recessive, males are affected more often then females.

X-linked dominant diseases include hypophosphatemia, a type of rickets. X-linked recessive diseases include color blindness, hemophilia, muscular dystrophy, and glucose-6-phosphate dehydrogenase deficiency. Y-linked disorders can only occur in males. In this case, the trait is transferred from father to son 100% of the time.

Mitochondria within each cell have their own DNA. Billions of years ago, ancestors of mitochondria were probably free-living cells that formed a symbiotic relationship with primitive human cells. Mitochondrial DNA aberrations can cause disease to occur. These diseases can only be genetically passed from the mother to the child.

A branch of genetics known as pharmacogenetics is concerned with genetic variation that underlies drug responses. Differences in drug responses can produce a range of phenotypic responses: drug resistance, toxic sensitivity to low doses, development of cancer after prolonged exposure, or an unexpected reaction to a combination of drugs. Some of these drug response variations are harmless, but some may be life threatening. In the future, drugs will be designed with the specific genetic phenotype of the person receiving the drug in mind. For example, cholinesterase reuptake inhibitors are used for patients with Alzheimer's dementia. These types of drugs are effective for those patients who have the E4 gene for Alzheimer's. The drug is not effective in those Alzheimer's patients who do not have the E4 gene. If we were able to perform routine testing for the E4 gene on Alzheimer's patients, we could prevent giving the drug to those for whom it would not be effective, reducing cost and the potential for side effects.

Nursing Situations in the Practice of Nursing Genetics

In this section, several nursing situations are presented. While none of the situations presented are from real life stories, they do represent frequent scenarios, problems, and issues of families in which genetic problems arise. Many of the ethical, legal, moral, physiological, and social issues are discussed. Questions asked at the end of the nursing situations are presented for reflection and discussion in small groups. Many do not have right or wrong answers, but rather are meant to assist the nurse in developing ways of thinking should situations like these present.

Case One

Mr. and Mrs. Salazar have just had their first baby, and you are the nurse caring for both mother and baby. Mrs. Salazar is 38 years old and a teacher. Mr. Salazar is also 38 and is an accountant. The day after delivery, the physician tells the parents that the child has trisomy 21 or Down's syndrome. They are unable to tell at this time how well the child will function; however, the child will have physical and mental deficiencies. The physicians also tells the parents that many Down's syndrome children live at home and thrive. Mr and Mrs. Salazar are sitting holding hands and Mrs. Salazar is quietly crying during the physician's discussion. The physicians then tell both parents that they should not ask questions right now but wait until they have had a chance to assimilate the information already given and read the printed information handed to them.

After the physicians leave, the nurse notes that Mr. and Mrs. Salazar are both crying. The nurse enters the room, takes Mrs. Salazar's hand, and asks what she can do for her now. The parents ask several questions:

- How did this happen?
- Why did it happen to our baby?
- What did we do to cause this to happen?
- Should we give up on the idea of ever having any more children?
- Could we have known about this earlier?

The nurse presents Mr. and Mrs. Salazar with some basic information about the genetic cause of Down's syndrome. The nurse shares with the Salazar's information about the increased risk of Down's syndrome in mothers over 35 years of age; they discuss the role of amniocentesis in the early diagnosis of congenital anomalies and the fact that it is difficult to tell whether subsequent pregnancies would have the same result.

Mrs. Salazar says that she declined amniocentesis because she would never have an abortion. If she had known, however, she thinks it would have been easier to know ahead of time even though she would have completed the pregnancy.

Reflective Questions:

- What are some things the nurse could do at this point to help the Salazar family adjust to this new baby?

- How can the nurse assess how well the mother and father react to the baby when it is brought to the room for feedings?

- What types of genetic counseling would benefit the Salazar family?

- What types of genetic counseling would benefit Mrs. Salazar's sister who is getting married next year and is 25 years old?

- How do you understand the mother, father, and baby as unique individuals and as a family unit?

- If baby Salazar is profoundly mentally handicapped, how could you as the nurse help the parents make a decision about how to care for the baby and still have productive and fulfilling lives?

Case 2

Mrs. Klinenschoen has been diagnosed with Huntington's chorea. She knows her mother had Huntington's chorea as well, and that as an autosomal recessive trait she had a 50% chance of having the gene for the disease. She also knows that if the Huntington's gene is present, it is expressed 100% of the time. Mrs. Klinenschoen decided as a young woman that she did not want to be tested for the gene because she did not want to live her life knowing she would get this dreadful disease. She felt it would keep her from fully experiencing her life as a young woman. Now Mrs. Klinenschoen has a daughter of her own who is 15 years old. Her daughter wants to be tested for the Huntington's gene, but her mother, as her legal guardian, will not allow her to be tested. The daughter is not emancipated and cannot have the test without her mother's approval.

- As the nurse in the clinic, how would you begin a dialogue with both of these women regarding the issue of the daughter being tested for Huntington's chorea?

- What considerations should the nurse reflect upon before beginning the discussion?

- Why do you think the daughter wants to be tested?

- Why does the mother not want the testing done?

- What are the rights of each legally, ethically, and morally in this situation?

- Can these conflicts be resolved?

- How will this genetic disorder affect future generations if Mrs. Klinenschoen's daughter decides to have children?

- How would you advise this 15-year-old woman?

Case 3

Mrs. Allen is six months into treatment for breast cancer and has tested positive for the BRACA 1 gene. The BRACA 1 gene in woman increases the risk for breast cancer by 75%. Mrs. Allen has two teenage sons and one teenage daughter, Lindsay, who is 12. She asks you as the nurse to speak to Lindsay about the predisposition for breast and ovarian cancers if she is positive for the BRACA 1 gene like her mother. She would like the nurse to "talk Lindsay into" being tested for the BRACA 1 gene. Her mother feels that if Lindsay tests negative, Mrs. Allen can relax, and if she does test positive, then at least the family can be very proactive in cancer prevention.

- Should you as the nurse "talk" Lindsay into having the test for "her own good"?

- What if Lindsay decides not to be tested?

- How will you work with the family who disagrees on genetic testing issues?

- What about Mrs. Allen's sons, should they be tested?

- What are some of the other ethical issues surrounding this type of testing (confidentiality, future ability to obtain health insurance)?

Summary

The science of genetics has the potential to transform healthcare outcomes. This has significant implications for both providers and consumers of healthcare. Nurses have a responsibility to become active participants in genetic education, practice, and policy. Translating genetic information into practical information for consumers requires nurses to become familiar with new terminology, concepts, and technologies. Nurses in their role as patient and family advocates must address ethical and social questions facing consumers of genetic healthcare. Evaluating strategies that effectively address ethical dilemmas in clinical practice should be a nursing focus.

Genetic information and technologies may greatly assist nurses to come to know each unique person for whom they care. Therefore, genetics presents both a blessing and a challenge. The blessing cannot be realized, and the challenges cannot be met, however, if nurses are unaware of the fast evolving field of knowledge.

Glossary

Affected: An individual who manifests symptoms of a particular condition.

Allele: One of the alternative versions of a gene at a given location (locus) along a chromosome.

Aneuploidy: The occurrence of one or more extra or missing chromosomes leading to an unbalanced chromosome complement, or, any chromosome number that is not an exact multiple of the haploid number.

Autosomal: Refers to any of the chromosomes other than the sex-determining chromosomes (i.e., the X and Y) or the genes on these chromosomes.

Autosomal (dominant): Describes a trait or disorder in which the phenotype is expressed in those who have inherited only one copy of a particular gene mutation (heterozygotes); specifically refers to a gene on one of the 22 pairs of autosomes (non-sex chromosomes).

Autosomal (recessive): Describes a trait or disorder requiring the presence of two copies of a gene mutation at a particular locus in order to express observable phenotype; specifically refers to genes on one of the 22 pairs of autosomes (non-sex chromosomes).

Base pair (bp): Two nitrogenous bases paired together in double-stranded DNA by weak bonds; specific pairing of these bases (adenine with thymine and guanine with cytosine) facilitates accurate DNA replication; when quantified (e.g., 8 bp), refers to the physical length of a sequence of nucleotides.

Carrier: An individual who has a recessive, disease-causing gene mutation at a particular locus on one chromosome of a pair and a normal allele at that locus on the other chromosome; may also refer to an individual with a balanced chromosome rearrangement.

Chromosome: Physical structure consisting of DNA and supporting proteins called chromatin. Human cells normally contain 46 chromosomes identified as 23 pairs; 22 pairs are autosomes and one pair are the sex chromosomes.

Congenital: Present from birth, but not necessarily genetic.

Consanguinity: Genetic relatedness between individuals descended from at least one common ancestor.

Correlation: The association between the presence of a certain mutation or mutations (genotype) and the resulting physical trait, abnormality, or pattern of abnormalities (phenotype). With respect to genetic testing, the frequency with which a certain phenotype is observed in the presence of a specific genotype determines the positive predictive value of the test.

DNA: (Synonym: deoxyribonucleic acid) The molecule which encodes the genes responsible for the structure and function of an organism and allows for transmission of genetic information from one generation to the next.

Dominant: See autosomal dominant or X-linked dominant.

Duplication: The presence of an extra segment of DNA, resulting in redundant copies of a portion of a gene, an entire gene, or a series of genes, usually caused by unequal crossing-over during gene replication when gametes are formed in meiosis.

Dysmorphology: The clinical study of malformation syndromes.

False Negative Result: A test result that indicates that an individual is unaffected and/or does not have a particular gene mutation when she or he is actually affected and/or does have a gene mutation; i.e., a negative test result in an affected individual.

False Positive Result: A test result that indicates that an individual is affected and/or has a certain gene mutation when she or he is actually unaffected and/or does not have the mutation; i.e., a positive test result in a truly unaffected individual.

Familial: A phenotype that occurs in more than one family member; may have genetic or non-genetic etiology.

Gene: The basic unit of heredity, consisting of a segment of DNA arranged in a linear manner along a chromosome, that codes for a specific protein or segment of protein leading to a particular characteristic or function.

Gene therapy: Experimental treatment of a genetic disorder that replaces, supplements, or manipulates the expression of abnormal genes with normally functioning genes.

Genetic Counseling: A process involving an individual or family, comprising: evaluation to confirm, diagnose, or exclusion of a genetic condition, malformation syndrome, or isolated birth defect; discussion of natural history and the role of heredity; identification of medical management issues; calculation and communication of genetic risks; provision of or referral for psychosocial support.

Genetic Predisposition: (Synonym: **genetic susceptibility**) Increased susceptibility to a particular disease due to the presence of one or more gene mutations associated with an increased risk for the disease and/or a family history that indicates an increased risk for the disease.

Genome: The complete DNA sequence, containing all genetic information and supporting proteins, in the chromosomes of an individual or species.

Genotype: The genetic constitution of an organism or cell; also refers to the specific set of alleles inherited at a locus.

Genotyping: Testing that reveals the specific alleles inherited by an individual; particularly useful for situations in which more than one genotypic combination can produce the same clinical presentation, as in the ABO blood group, where both the AO and AA genotypes yield type A blood.

Haploid: Half the diploid or normal number of chromosomes in a somatic cell; the number of chromosomes in a gamete (egg or sperm) cell, which in humans is 23 chromosomes, one chromosome from each chromosome pair.

Hemizygous: Describes an individual who has only one member of a chromosome pair or chromosome segment rather than the usual two; refers in particular to X-linked genes in males who under usual circumstances have only one X chromosome.

Heterozygote: With respect to a particular trait or condition, an individual who has inherited two different alleles, usually one normal and the other abnormal at a particular locus.

Homologous Chromosomes: (Synonym: **homologs**) The two chromosomes from a particular pair, normally one inherited from the mother and one from the father, containing the same genetic loci in the same order.

Homozygote: With respect to a particular trait or condition, an individual who has inherited identical alleles at a particular locus.

Incidence: The rate at which new cases occur, often expressed as number of new cases per number of live births.

Insertion: A chromosome abnormality in which material from one chromosome is inserted into another nonhomologous chromosome; a mutation in which a segment of DNA is inserted into a gene or other segment of DNA, potentially disrupting the coding sequence.

Inversion: A chromosomal rearrangement in which a segment of a chromosome has inverted from end to end and re-inserted into the chromosome at the same breakage site. Balanced inversions (in which no net loss or gain of genetic material occurs) are usually not associated with phenotypic abnormalities, however, in some cases, gene disruptions at the breakpoints can cause adverse phenotypic effects, including some known genetic diseases. Unbalanced inversions (in which loss or gain of chromosome material occurs) nearly always yield an abnormal phenotype.

Karyotype: A photographic representation of the chromosomes of a single cell, cut and arranged in pairs based on their banding pattern and size according to a standard classification.

Marker: An identifiable segment of DNA (e.g., RFLP, VNTR, microsatellite) with enough variation between individuals that its inheritance and co-inheritance with alleles of a given gene can be traced; used in linkage analysis.

Mitochondrial Inheritance: Mitochondria, cytoplasmic organelles that produce the energy source ATP for most chemical reactions in the body, contain their own distinct genome; mutations in mitochondrial genes are responsible for several recognized syndromes and are always maternally inherited since ova contain mitochondria, whereas sperm do not.

Mode of Inheritance: (Synonyms: inheritance pattern, pattern of inheritance) The manner in which a particular genetic trait or disorder is passed from one generation to the next. Autosomal dominant, autosomal recessive, X-linked dominant, X-linked recessive, multifactorail, and mitrochondrial inheritance are examples.

Molecular Genetic Testing: (Synonyms: DNA-based testing, DNA testing, molecular testing) Testing that involves the analysis of DNA, either through linkage analysis, sequencing, or one of several methods of mutation detection.

Monosomy: The presence of only one chromosome from a pair; partial monosomy refers to the presence of only one copy of a segment of a chromosome.

Mutation: (Synonym: sequence alteration) Any alteration in a gene from its natural state; may be benign (commonly referred to as a "polymorphism"), pathogenic, or of unknown significance.

Newborn Screening: Testing done within days of birth to identify infants at increased risk for a specific genetic disorder so that treatment can begin as soon as possible; when a newborn screening result is positive, further diagnostic testing is usually required to confirm or specify the results and counseling is offered to educate the parents.

Obligate Carrier: (Synonym: **obligate heterozygote**) An individual who may be clinically unaffected but who must carry a gene mutation based on analysis of the family history; usually applies to disorders inherited in an autosomal recessive and X-linked recessive manner.

PCR (Polymerase chain reaction): A procedure that produces millions of copies of a short segment of DNA through repeated cycles of: 1) denaturation, 2) annealing, and 3) elongation; PCR is a very common procedure in molecular genetic testing and may be used to: 1) generate a sufficient quantity of DNA to perform a test (e.g., sequence analysis, mutation scanning), or 2) may be a test in and of itself (e.g., allele-specific amplification, trinucleotide repeat quantification).

Pedigree: A diagram of the genetic relationships and medical history of a family using standardized symbols and terminology.

Penetrance: The proportion of individuals with a mutation causing a particular disorder who exhibit clinical symptoms of that disorder; most often refers to autosomal dominant conditions.

Phenotype: The observable physical and/or biochemical characteristics of the expression of a gene; the clinical presentation of an individual with a particular genotype.

Polymorphism: (Synonym: polymorphic allele) Natural variations in a gene, DNA sequence, or chromosome that have no adverse effects on the individual and occur with fairly high frequency in the general population.

Polyploidy: An increase in the number of haploid sets (23) of chromosomes in a cell. **Triploidy:** Refers to three whole sets of chromosomes in a single cell (in humans, a total of 69 chromosomes per cell).

Tetraploidy: Refers to four whole sets of chromosomes in a single cell (in humans, a total of 92 chromosomes per cell).

Population Risk: (Synonym: **background risk**) The proportion of individuals in the general population who are affected with a particular disorder or who carry a certain gene; often discussed in the genetic counseling process as a comparison to the patient's personal risk given her or his family history or other circumstances.

Prevalence: The number of cases per size of the population at a given time.

Proband: (Synonyms: index case, **propositus**) The affected individual through whom a family with a genetic disorder is ascertained; may or may not be the consultand (the individual presenting for genetic counseling).

Sensitivity: The frequency with which a test yields a positive result when the individual being tested is actually affected and/or has the gene mutation in question.

Sequence Alteration: (Synonym: **mutation**) Any alteration in a gene from its natural state; may be benign (commonly referred to as a "polymorphism"), pathogenic, or of unknown significance.

Susceptibility: The possible genetic predisposition toward a disease or genetic trait.

Gene: (Synonym: **predisposing mutation**) A gene mutation that increases the likelihood that an individual will develop a certain disease or disorder. When such a mutation is inherited, development of symptoms is more likely but not certain.

Telomere: The segment at the end of each chromosome arm which consists of a series of repeated DNA sequences that regulate chromosomal replication at each cell division. Some of the telomere is lost each time a cell divides, and eventually, when the telomere is gone, the cell dies.

Translocation: (Synonym: **chromosome rearrangement**) A chromosome alteration in which a whole chromosome or segment of a chromosome becomes attached to or interchanged with another whole chromosome or segment, the resulting hybrid segregating together at meiosis; balanced translocations (in which there is no net loss or gain of chromosome material) are usually not associated with phenotypic abnormalities, although gene disruptions at the breakpoints of the translocation can, in some cases, cause adverse effects, including some known genetic disorders; unbalanced translocations (in which there is loss or gain of chromosome material) nearly always yield an abnormal phenotype.

Trisomy: The presence of a single extra chromosome, yielding a total of three chromosomes of that particular type instead of a pair. Partial trisomy refers to the presence of an extra copy of a segment of a chromosome.

Unaffected: An individual who does not manifest any symptoms of a particular condition

Variable: The different ways in which a gene can be expressed in a human.

Expression: Variation in clinical features (type and severity) of a genetic disorder between individuals with the same gene alteration, even within the same family.

X-linked Dominant: Describes a dominant trait or disorder caused by a mutation in a gene on the X chromosome. The phenotype is expressed in heterozygous females as well as in hemizygous males (having only one X chromosome); affected males tend to have a more severe phenotype than affected females.

X-linked Recessive: A mode of inheritance in which a mutation in a gene on the X chromosome causes the phenotype to be expressed in males who are hemizygous for the gene mutation (i.e., they have only one X chromosome) and in females who are homozygous for the gene mutation (i.e., they have a copy of the gene mutation on each of their two X chromosomes). Carrier females who have only one copy of the mutation do not usually express the phenotype, although differences in X-chromosome inactivation can lead to varying degrees of clinical expression in carrier females.

(Definitions from **http://www.ncbi.nlm.nih.gov/genome/guide/human/**)

Table 11.1.   Recommendations for genetic education for all healthcare professionals.

KNOWLEDGE: All healthcare professionals should know:

Basic genetic terminology.

Basic patterns of biological inheritance.

Diseases associated with genetic variations.

Role of genetic factors in maintaining health and preventing disease.

Identification of genetic predisposition to disease.

The role of behavioral, social, and environmental factors to modify or influence genetics

The influence of culture, ethnicity, health beliefs, and economics on the ability to use genetic information.

Resources available to assist clients seek genetic information.

Indications for referral to genetic specialists.

Indications for genetic testing and/or gene based interventions.

Ethical, legal, and social issues related to genetic testing and recording of information.

The history of misuse of genetic information.

The professional's role in referral to genetics services, provision, follow-up, and quality review of genetic services.

ATTITUDES: All healthcare professionals should:

Recognize philosophical, theological, cultural, and ethical perspectives influencing the use of genetic information and services.

Appreciate the sensitivity of genetic information and the need for privacy and confidentiality.

Recognize the importance of delivering genetic education and counseling.

Demonstrate willingness to update genetic knowledge at frequent intervals.

Support patient-focused policies.

continues

Table 11.1.   Recommendations for genetic education for all healthcare professionals.   (continued)

SKILLS: All healthcare professionals should be able to:

Gather genetic family history information, including an appropriate multigenerational family history.

Identify clients who would benefit from genetic services.

Explain basic concepts of genetics and the influence of genetic factors in health maintenance.

Participate in professional and public education about genetics.

Educate patients about the availability of genetic testing.

Provide information about the potential risks, benefits, and limitations of genetic testing.

Discuss the wide range of emotional effects of genetic diseases on individuals and family members.

Safeguard privacy and confidentiality of genetic information.

Inform patients of potential limitations to maintain privacy and confidentiality of fgnetic information.

Table 11.2.   List of Diseases that can be diagnosed through prenatal testing.

Diseases that can be diagnosed by prenatal testing.

Acatalasemia

Adrenogential syndrome

Chediak-Higashi syndrome

Citrullinemia

Cystathioninuria

Systic fibrosis

Fabry disease

Fucosidosis

Galactosemia

Gaucher disease

G6PD deficiency

Diseases that can be diagnosed by prenatal testing. *(continued)*

Homocystinuria
I-cell disease
Lesch-Nyhan syndrome
Mannosidosis
Maple syrup urine disease
Marfan syndrome
Muscular Dystrophy
Niemann-Pick Disease
Oroticaciduria
Progeria
Sandhoff Disease
Spina Bifida
Tay-Sachs Disease
Thalessemia
Werner Syndrome
Xeroderma Pigmentosa

References

American Nurses Association. (1998). *Statement on the scope and standards of genetics clinical nursing practice.* Washington, DC: American Nurses Publishing.

American Nurses Association. (1999). *Code of ethics for nurses with interpretive statements.* Washington, DC: American Nurses Publishing.

Andrews, L., Fullarton, J., Holtzman, N., & Motulsky A. (1994). *Assessing genetic risks: Implications for health and social policy.* Washington, DC: American Association of Colleges of Nursing.

Collins, F. (2004) Genetics and nursing science. Nursing Research. 52(2) 3-6.

International Society of Nurses in Genetics. (1998). *Statement on the scope and standards of genetics clinical nursing practice.* Washington, DC: American Nursing Association.

Jenkins, J., & Collins, F. (2003). Are you genetically literate? *American Journal of Nursing, 103*(4), 13-15.

Lea, D., Jenkins, J., Francomano, C., & Francomano, C. (1998). *Genetics in clinical practice: New directions for nursing and healthcare.* Boston: Jones & Bartlett.

The Human Genome Project: *http://www.ncbi.nlm.nih.gov/genome/ guide/human/*

Williams, J. (2002). Education for genetics and nursing practice. *AACN Clinical Issues, 13*(4), 492-500.

PART

Resources

APPENDIX

Ontological and Epistemological Questions

Supported by Technological Competency as Caring: A Model for Practice

The following are ontological and epistemological questions of nursing that are designed to enhance the appreciation of the tension between practicing nursing and the practice of nursing as understood from another disciplinary perspective:

- Should nursing knowledge be grounded in empirical data?
- Should nursing be like medicine? If so, why?
- Should nursing *not* be like medicine? If so, why?
- Is the focus of nursing the health or wellness of persons?
- In attempting to attain, maintain, and sustain the health and wellness of persons, do nurses need to understand what it is like to be a person?
- Are nurses meeting the desired outcomes of attaining, maintaining, and sustaining the health and wellness of persons when they practice like physicians?
- From an advanced perspective of nursing as medicine, can the nurse provide healthcare from a more affordable position?
- If nursing is like medicine, if nursing practice is like medical practice, if by this practice the nurse focuses on the person as whole and complete in the moment, and is able to attain, maintain, and sustain health and well-being of the person, is the nurse nursing?
- If the nurse is nursing, and the person is being nursed, and the health and wellness of persons is attained, maintained, and sustained, then is nursing meeting the societal need of a profession, a service profession?

APPENDIX

Biographical Profiles of Contributing Authors

Alan Barnard, RN, BA, MA, PhD, is senior lecturer at the School of Nursing, Queensland University of Technology in Brisbane, Australia. He has qualifications in nursing, psychology, education, and philosophy. He has been involved in clinical practice and nurse education for more than 20 years and has extensive research and scholarly experience. His research and scholarly interests relate to the education of nurses and the human experience of technology, with particular emphasis on critical examination of beliefs and assumptions that inform understanding of technology and nursing. He currently holds the position of course coordinator for the bachelor of nursing, Queensland University of Technology, Australia.

Aric S. Campling, RN, MS, earned his bachelor of science in nursing at Georgetown University in Washington, D.C., and his master of science with a focus in nursing administration at Florida Atlantic University's Christine E. Lynn College of Nursing in Boca Raton, Florida. Mr. Campling spent the first few years of his nursing career as a cardiac care/telemetry nurse in Maryland and then in Boynton Beach, Florida. He is currently a clinical systems analyst for a community hospital and plans to seek ANCC certification in nursing informatics. Mr. Campling's academic interests mesh with his professional role and revolve around theories of nursing, caring, change, and information technology.

Patrick J. Dean, RN, BSN, MSN, has a background of 30 years in nursing. His practice has been devoted primarily to young persons. He has worked with ante-partum high risk patients at Rush University in Chicago, Illinois, and has spent almost 20 years in child and adolescent psychiatry at the Mayo Foundation in Rochester, Minnesota. Prior to his formal nursing career, Patrick volunteered with various U.S. and U.K. organizations. He has received several healthcare awards, including outstanding alumnus from his alma mater, Minnesota State University, Mankato, Minnesota. His research is primarily in human caring and preventive healthcare.

Rozzano C. Locsin, RN, PhD, is professor of nursing at Florida Atlantic University's Christine E. Lynn College of Nursing in Boca Raton, Florida. He holds a master's degree from Silliman University and a doctor of philosophy in nursing from the University of the Philippines. He was a Fulbright Scholar to Uganda in 2000 and is a recipient of the 2004-2006 Fulbright Alumni Initiative Award. He has been listed as a Fulbright Senior Specialist in the field of Global Health and International Development since December 2004. He edited the quintessential book, *Advancing Technology, Caring and Nursing* in 2001 and is co-editor of the book *Technology and Nursing Practice* to be published by Palgrave Macmillan Ltd. in 2005. In 2003, he received the prestigious Edith Moore Copeland Excellence in Creativity Award from The Honor Society of Nursing, Sigma Theta Tau International. He is a recipient of two lifetime achievement awards in nursing education. Dr. Locsin's international work includes curriculum development in master and doctoral nursing education programs in Uganda, Thailand, and the Philippines. In addition, he collaborates with colleagues on scholarly and creative projects in Australia, Hong Kong, the Philippines, Thailand, and Uganda. He has published nationally and internationally, pursuing projects and programs on topics about holistic nursing, care of older persons, alternative and complementary therapies, and health promotion and early intervention. "Life transformations and transitions in the health-illness experience" defines his research, and knowing persons through technology, caring, and nursing is his passion.

Ruth McCaffrey, ND; ARNP, received her nursing doctorate from Case Western Reserve University in Cleveland, Ohio, and is an assistant professor of nursing at Florida Atlantic University's Christine E Lynn College of Nursing where she is also the director of the Initiative for Intentional Health. In addition to teaching, Dr. McCaffrey practices as a nurse practitioner in private practice in West Palm Beach, Florida. Dr. McCaffrey participated in a genetics training program at Cincinnati Children's Hospital in 2001. During that time, she was able to participate in exploring the latest in genetic information and the impact genetics has on advanced practice nursing. As a nurse practitioner, Dr. McCaffrey holds ANCC certifications in both family and geriatric practice. Dr. McCaffrey has published widely in journals and books on subjects such as advanced practice nursing, pain management, and the use of the arts in healing.

Marguerite J. Purnell, RN, PhD, is assistant professor at Florida Atlantic University's Christine E Lynn College of Nursing, Boca Raton, Florida. She earned her bachelor of science in nursing and her master of science in nursing at Florida Atlantic University and her PhD in nursing from the University of Miami. Having spent her formative years in New Zealand, she brings to nursing the rich cultural perspectives of the South Pacific. Her research interests include nursing philosophy, the expression of intentionality in nursing, and the articulation of theory-based practice from a caring perspective. Dr. Purnell believes that in addition to excellence in practice, nurses must be able to professionally negotiate and communicate caring within an interdisciplinary context, not only regionally, but on a national and global scale.

Savina O. Schoenhofer, RN, PhD, has been a professor and a faculty member with the School of Nursing at Alcorn State University since 1996. She teaches in the Department of Graduate Nursing. Previous appointments have included Texas Tech University, University of Mississippi, Florida Atlantic University, and Wichita State University. Dr. Schoenhofer is co-developer of the theory of Nursing as Caring (www.nursingascaring.com) and co-author of the book, *Nursing As Caring: A Model for Transforming Practice.* Dr. Schoenhofer is co-founder of the occasional publication, *Nightingale Songs,* a charter member of the International Association for Human Caring and has been actively engaged in the study of caring since 1983, with many professional publications in this field. Her research interests lie in two complementary areas: everyday caring and outcomes of caring in nursing. A focus of her research has been the development of inquiry approaches specific to the study of the theory of Nursing as Caring. A native Kansan, Dr. Schoenhofer received both her bachelor of science in nursing and her master's in nursing from Wichita State University. She earned her PhD from Kansas State University.

Index

U–V

W–X–Y–Z

The *New* Virginia Henderson International Nursing Library

ceLink™

One price for all the CE you need

When you need contact hours for personal growth, licensure or certification, go to www.nursingsociety.org/ceonline and choose from a wide variety of peer-reviewed, self-study learning activities.

These online courses developed by the Honor Society of Nursing, Sigma Theta Tau International support and enhance your ability to make critical decisions while managing complex health care situations.

Topics include:
- Adult Health
- Cardiovascular
- Disaster Readiness
- Ethics
- Evidence-Based Nursing
- Genetics
- Infectious Disease
- Leadership/Management

- Obstetrics
- Oncology
- Pain Management
- Palliative Care
- Pediatrics
- Personal Development
- Psychiatric/Mental Health
- Women's Health

New!

For a one-time fee, ceLink™ gives you 12 months of unlimited access* to case studies and articles.
*not available on all courses

Prices are as low as $19.95
Institutional prices available—call 888.NKI.4.YO

ceLink™ and the comprehensive offerings of nurseAdvance™ Knowledge Solutions have been developed by the Honor Society of Nursing, Sigma Theta Tau International and are brought to you through its subsidiary, Nursing Knowledge International™.

Register today at www.nursingsociety.org/ceonline

Sigma Theta Tau International
Honor Society of Nursing
IMPROVING WORLD HEALTH THROUGH KNOWLEDGE™

The honor society is accredited to provide continuing nursing education by the American Nurses Credentialing Center's Commission on Accreditation.